Welcome ladies and gentlemen to the second issue of Scenes, a publication I put together every few months between music, book and film projects. This issue covers a wide range of areas from the history of classic and cult cinema. There is an interview with actress Bernice Stegers who recalls her experiences of working on Fellini's City of Women. There is also a chat with Scott Anthony about his time with Ken Russell on Savage Messiah. But most of the issue is dedicated to two immortal Hollywood legends, Sophia Loren and Marilyn Monroe, exploring these two remarkable women and the wonderful pictures they made in the fifties and sixties. I hope you enjoy reading through and find something that tickles your fancy...

- Editor, Chris Wade.

CONTENTS

I0510402

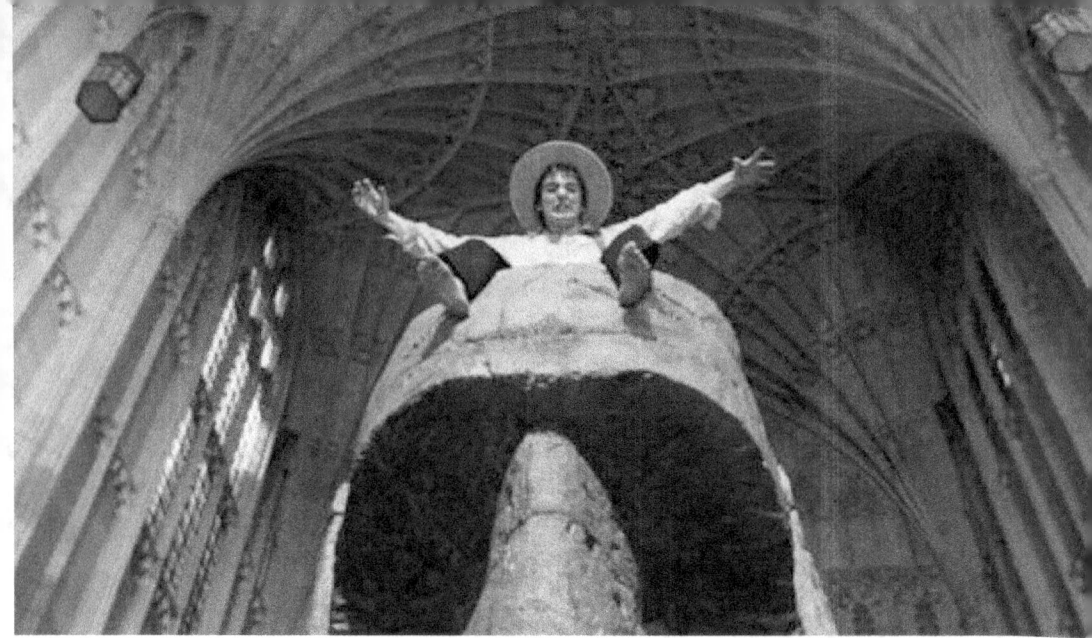

SAVAGE MESSIAH
SCOTT ANTHONY ON WORKING WITH KEN RUSSELL
ON AN OVERLOOKED MASTERPIECE

Ken Russell really was THE British director of the early 1970s, and his films were long running cinema staples in the West End. Consider the run of films up to The Boy Friend; Women In Love, The Music Lovers, The Devils, not to mention his shocking and outrageous BBC film Dance of the Seven Veils - and you have one of the most stunning runs in the history of British cinema. "Even when his films were shocking they were always successful," his friend and collaborator Melvyn Bragg once said, a telling statement that really defined Russell's success in that era.

But the truth was, the establishment weren't going to love Ken forever. He was too wild, exuberant and stubborn to play the game, and as the decade went on, his films seemed to get more feral, ridiculous, over the top and, it has to be said, perhaps often purposely controversial. Ken was film's naughty boy, an upstart who loved brewing up trouble, then standing back and watching it all unfold with great amusement. To him, excess was king, and he went wherever his instinct took him.

The rest of the 1970s were taken up by varied film projects, Savage Messiah being the first of these, released in 1972. Now one of his least celebrated films, it's been buried in time somewhat; which is a shame, as his biopic on the French sculptor Henri Gaudier is actually a very enjoyable Russellian biopic, though more toned down than, say, Mahler or Lisztomania. Scott Anthony plays the lead, a man juggling with the duality of deep relationships and the commitments of living as a pure artist. It turned out to be one of Russell's most sympathetic biographical films, an understated affair (for Ken at least) that celebrated the creative spirit. Based on the H S Ede biography on Gaudier, itself put together from Gaudier's letters to Sophie, here played by Dorothy Tutin, Ken paints him as a bohemian outlaw, charming

and likeable with a passion for life. "Art is alive," he declares. "Enjoy it, love it, or hate it, but don't worship it!" It's one of the most fitting lines in any Ken Russell film, and sounds like a statement from the man himself. Art is important, but it's not precious or above a laugh or two. As the man who had The Who's Roger Daltrey pick out groupies in Lisztomania with a gigantic penis, pointing it in their faces as he selects his next sexual partner, Ken knew this all too well.

You can also learn a lot about Ken from the poster for Savage Messiah alone, which proudly declared, "All art is sex." Was Gaudier Ken's one true screen alter ego? Whether he was or not, Savage Messiah was a film about art, not just the poetic romanticism of art, but the hard work, the hustling, the selling and the frustrations of finding the gold amidst the dross.

"I want to take the 'mystique' away from art," Ken said at the time the film was released, "and show that success is usually 5 per cent inspiration and 95 per cent perspiration and hard slog."

He succeeded in making Savage Messiah a film about the process of creation, highlighting the ups and downs of an artist's life. The artist willingly walks down his own path and should not be pitied, admired or frowned upon for his choice to exist outside society's structural constraints. No one owes him a living either, and luck will bring success if the time is right.

Savage Messiah is definitely one of the more low key offerings Ken came up with in his whole career, even though it does have its wilder moments, particularly a very memorable scene with a young Helen Mirren doing topless karate moves in a lavish mansion. There was still the trademark Russell direction in there, the jolts and zooms, but otherwise, he seemed to be on something of a creative leash. It was a character film, more about the people than the visual technique. Still, it didn't stop some critics having a go at him.

"Russell takes the mystique away from art, but supplies nothing much in its place," whined Vincent Canby of the New York Times. As the final contradiction, Canby finishes his review by admitting "Savage Messiah is so tame that it almost makes one long for the excesses of the earlier Russell films, which so overwhelmed the senses as to become anaesthetically soothing, like loud rock. At one point in the film, I had the feeling that perhaps Russell was really taking stock of his career to date." Had Ken made Savage Messiah another over the top, lavish, garish, bad taste bonanza, they'd have ripped it to shreds. You just can't win.

Here is my interview with Scott Anthony, star of Savage Messiah. Bits of this were used in my 2019 documentary on Ken, but printed below is the chat in full...

Do you remember how you got the part in the film?

Um.... Well I was at RADA. I was leaving actually and it was Christmas of 1970, or 71. I started to audition and that was one of them. This led to two or three more auditions. There

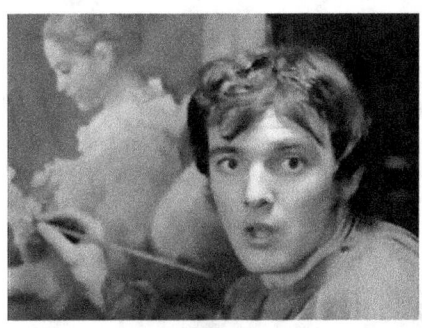

was another guy in the running too, from RADA as well. Me and him were down to the last two and somehow or other I got it!

What are your memories of first meeting Ken Russell?

I don't remember the very first meeting. As I say the auditions were quite intense. Ken had a lot of ideas of what he was looking for. For me, a young actor, I just wanted to be authentic. My relationship with Ken was never an intellectual one. He was a very established figure, I was brand new. But it became very workman like between us, in the best sense, as opposed to a social one at all. So I don't recall lots of meals and chats or anything. I must have done

something in the audition which he wanted. It became a three way relationship between Gaudier, Ken and me. The more I learned about him the more I admired him and his work, Gaudier that is. His work had always been an influence to me as it had Ken too.

So Ken was at his peak really wasn't he at this point? Was he fairly flamboyant to work for?

He had that exuberant side to him, but that did not come out in a social way or an over the top directorial way. It was very much to do with the part. There are scenes in the film which are very exuberant and were challenging to do, but as I say you had to get on Ken's wave length. I do not recall him asking me to give him less, usually more. Savage Messiah was a smaller film compared to others he'd made, fairly small and modest in scale. So I think this fact made it easier for him to have a focus and be clearer without the distractions of the big budgets and the stars that were on the bigger films.

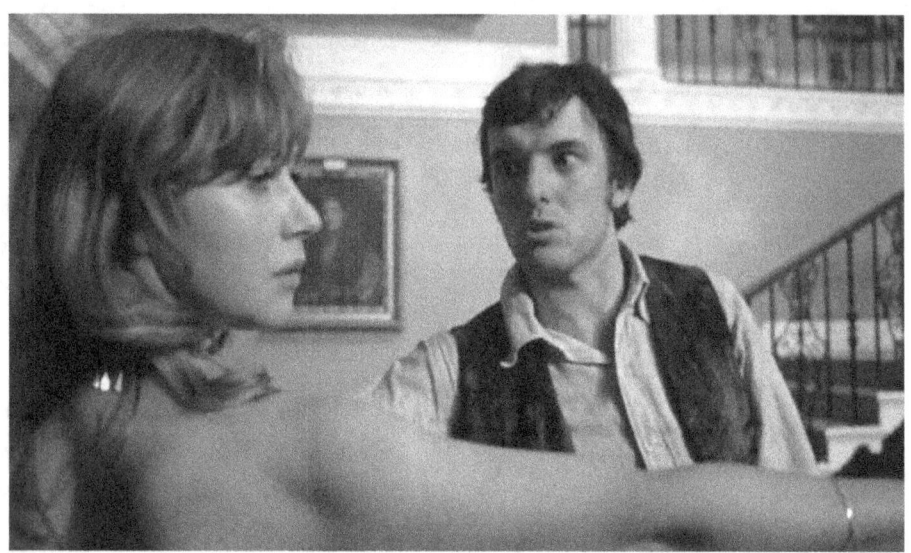

So the film came to have a focus, and a sincerity to it. Ken later found it to be one of his happiest times making a film. He was entirely able to focus on what he wanted to do. That was entirely where he was at. There wasn't much of that exuberance one had read about Ken. It wasn't like that. I have no memories of it being wild at all.

Yes, now it comes across as one of his more straight forward films doesn't it?

Yeah. I can remember riving about on the top of an Easter Island head. It was 20 foot high and made out of polystyrene. I do remember Ken demonstrating what he wanted to me. So that exuberance was there, that intensity as you will. It was in the doing of the work, rather than anything surrounding it. There is a scene at the end of the film where there is an exhibition of Gaudier's work after he's dead, and I found that a very emotional scene. It was done in a very straight forward way. But because of all the stuff before, in Gaudier's life as demonstrated by Ken, it has a certain intensity to it which I

6

felt represented not only Gaudier but Ken Russell himself.

Do you ever get people mentioning the film to you these days?

No I don't actually, it is rather obscure. It pops up every now and then. In 2014 they had a special showing at the BFI. I don't find it dated or anything. It has Russell characteristics to t, but a sincerity to it that continues. I know he said it was one of his favourite films he'd made. I think Ken has a lot of empathy with Gaudier's work. It's not hard to see the cross over between Gaudier and Ken's work. I saw Gaudier's work again recently, and the force of it was still there as it had been all those years ago.

Did working with Ken leave a lasting impression on you?

Yes. It was a very one off sort of experience, because he was very much out on a limb. It was not an intellectual approach to the whole thing. We did not have chats about motivation and various actory things. He was a unique character and working with him was a unique experience. I am very happy to have had the opportunity to work with him and to be introduced to that character and had the chance to share Ken's representation of the character who I always found to be influential. And working with Dorothy Tutin, that was a pleasure too.

What about working with Helen Mirren too? Did you enjoy that experience?

Well if you've seen the scene I had with her, how could you not? (Laughs) So yes I did, but she was an actor with a capital A. She had a lot of experience too. But Dorothy Tutin was playing a quieter character. Yet Helen Mirren, looking back, I certainly remember her more for the part she played, undoubtedly.

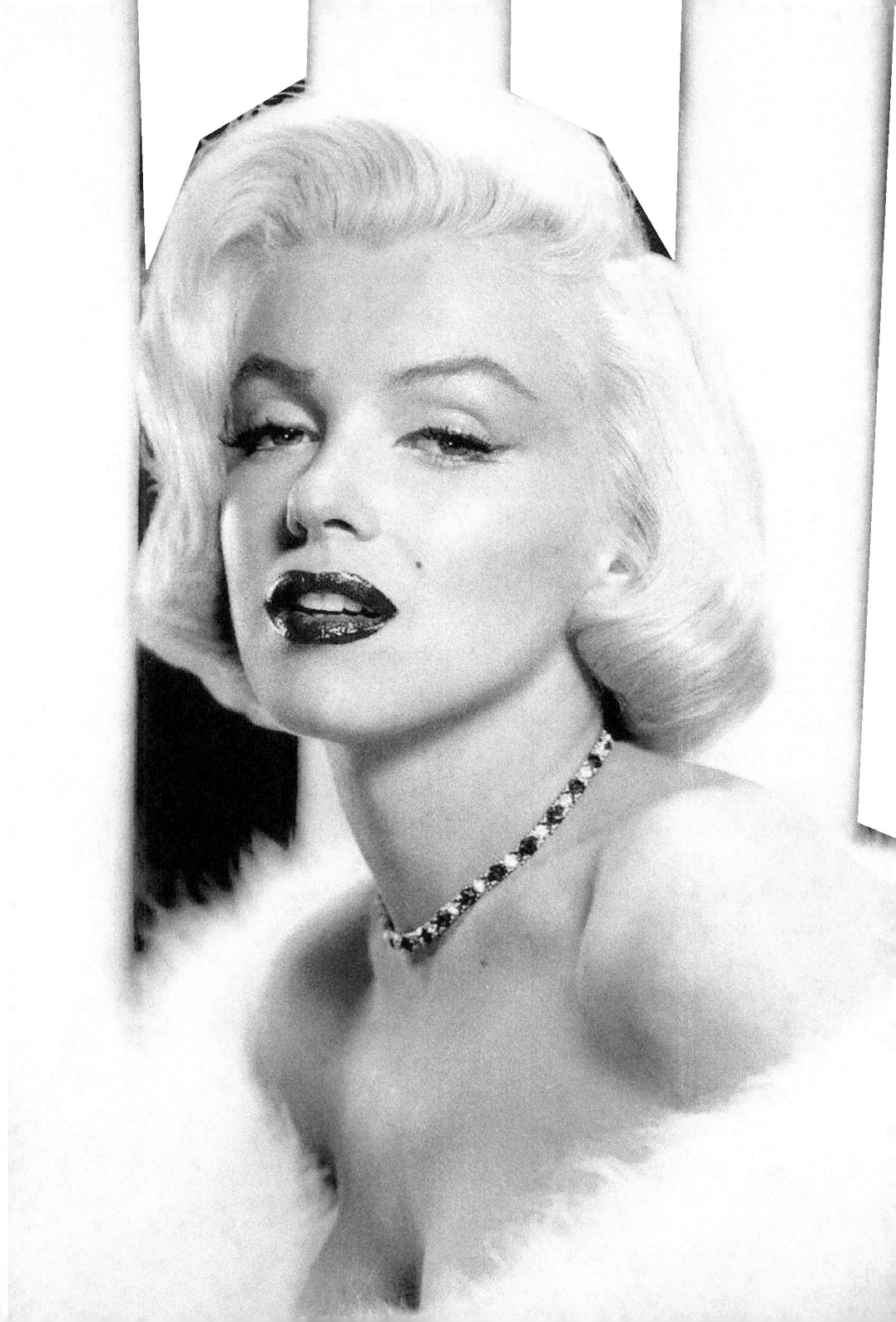

MARILYN MONROE

REMEMBERING THE ICON AND THE MAGIC SHE CREATED ON SCREEN

No one has had their life dissected and pulled apart quite as much as Marilyn Monroe. She is beyond legendary, beyond iconic, and her name alone has entered a myth of its own. Her face too, as familiar now as ever before, exists in that category exclusive to the higher ranks of 20th century icons; James Dean, Elvis Presley and John Lennon. Marilyn though, is in her own league. She is perhaps the most loved film star of all time, and her influence only seems to expand as the decades roll by. Let us not forget, she has been dead for almost sixty years now, yet that face of hers is remains ever so prominent in our collective consciousness. Hundreds if not thousands of books have been written about Monroe, about her life, her loves, her controversial times and her murky death. Less though, it has to be said, have focused on the very thing that made her famous in the first place - her film career.

There have of course been film guides released in the past, often largely illustrated editions, and biographies have indeed covered her movies. In recent times though, it seems that most of interest in Marilyn focuses on her final days, her depression, her sad childhood, her

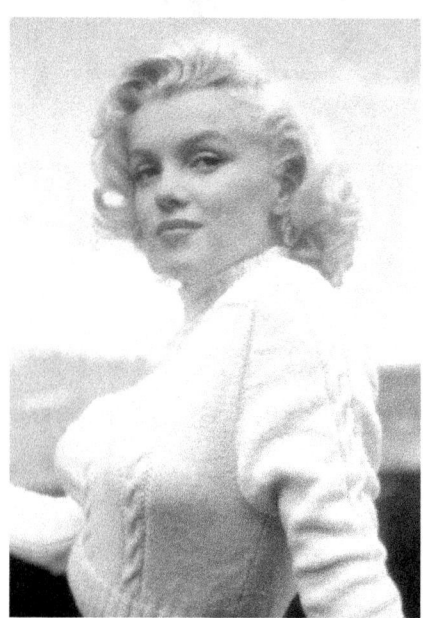

marriages to such people as Joe DiMaggio and Arthur Miller, her affairs with well known figures in politics, and her strange exit from this world, which itself has inspired countless conspiracy theories, each one more ludicrous than the last. What too often gets ignored though, or at least overlooked, are those marvellous films and the often magnificent performances she gave in them.

Again, when people do talk of Marilyn in the movies it's the familiar images, the magic moments which have entered film legend and helped engrave her into history; think the Diamonds Are A Girl's Best Friend sequence in 1953's Gentlemen Prefer Blondes; or the famous skirt-blowing scene in 1955's The Seven Year Itch. There is, of course, much more to her film career than these legendary moments though, and Monroe's filmography is full of gems. Some Like It Hot (1959) remains one of the most beloved comedies of all time, and Marilyn's role in it (alongside Tony Curtis and Jack Lemmon, dragging it up as part of a female touring group to hide from mobsters) as Sugar "Kane" Kowalczyk has become the epitome of sex appeal in movies. Again though, Marilyn was much more than an embodiment of sex, as proven in such features as River of No Return, The Prince and the Showgirl, and her final film, The Misfits (1961), which featured her deepest and most complex performance, a tragic yet fitting swan song for the most

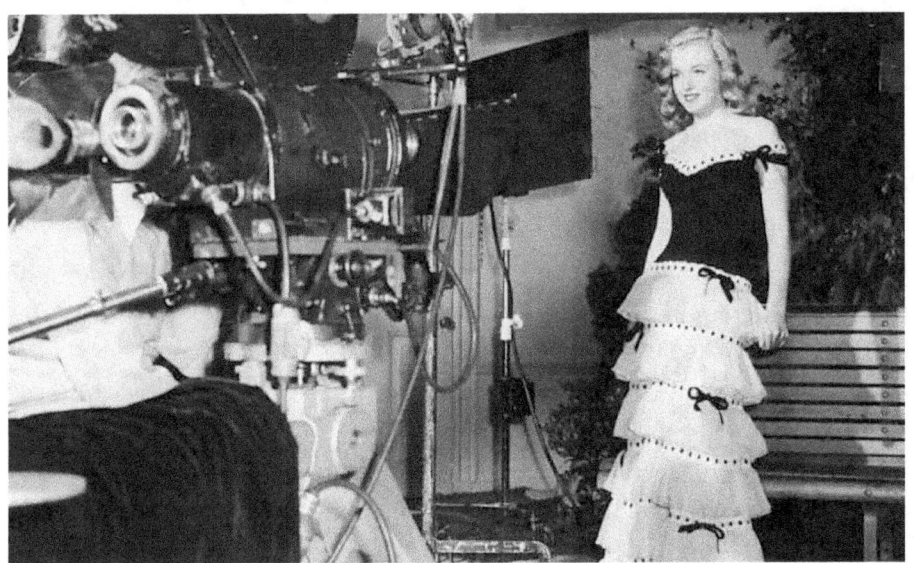

popular female star of mid-century cinema.

It is understandable at least that Marilyn's movies should be overshadowed by her life, given how turbulent and admittedly fascinating it was. She was born Norma Jeane Mortenson in Los Angeles, June 1 1926. Gladys Pearl Baker was her mother, though Marilyn never did find out who her biological father was. Clearly unable to look after her young daughter, Gladys sent young Norma to Albert and Ida Bolender, a kind couple who fostered her, though she moved back into a house with her mother when she was seven. But Gladys was mentally unstable and often found herself in mental care, while young Norma stayed with her mum's friend Grace. It was at this stage that Norma's life became troubled. She spent time living with her mother's old lodgers, the Atkinsons, and was sexually abused. By the age of ten she was being passed round various families and eventually ended up on Los Angeles Orphans Home. It was a brief stay, and she was taken in by Edwin and Grace Goddard, though this in itself was a short stay because it was revealed that Edwin was abusing Norma.

Naturally, this shy and retiring girl, who felt unwanted and dissatisfied - if not scared - of her own reality, retreated into make believe. In a 1962 interview with Life Magazine, Marilyn said "When I was five I think, that's when I started wanting to be an actress. I didn't like the world around me because it was kind of grim, but I loved to play house. When I heard that this was acting, I said that's what I want to be. Some of my foster families used to send me to the movies to get me out of the house and there I'd sit all day and way into the night. Up in front, there with the screen so big, a little kid all alone, and I loved it."

She settled down somewhat in the care of Ana Lower in Sawtelle, and began to frequent school. In 1942, while still only 18, she married the neighbour's son, James Dougherty. It was largely a marriage of convenience, for if not married Norma might have ended up back at the orphanage. Though a decent young man, there was no chance of them staying together. She famously remarked much later that she was "dying of boredom" while living with him.

When James went off with the Navy in 1944, Norma moved in with his parents. It was when working at a munitions factory that she was spotted by a photographer, David Conover, who saw something special in the young lady. Quitting her job, she was taken on by Conover and other photographers and began her career as a model. In 1947, after ditching Norma Jeane and stepping out as the more impressive sounding Marilyn Monroe, she was noticed by 20th Century Fox and taken on as a contract player.

But Marilyn's hopes of film success did not materialise, at least not yet. She landed some small movie roles, and her six month contract was extended. After appearing in Dangerous Years (1947) and Scudda Hoo! Scudda Hey! (1948), she realised that it would be a good idea to get some proper acting lessons, and Fox agreed to send her to the Actors' Laboratory Theatre. Marilyn loved her time there and it gave her a hunger to improve her screen acting skills. "I was hooked," she later said.

Unfortunately, Fox were not interested in renewing her contract, yet she stayed single minded in her quest for film stardom. She'd divorced her husband, continued to study at the lab and even landed some theatre experience in the play, Glamour Preferred. She made sure she was seen in the right places with the right people, going to Hollywood functions and befriending such people as gossip columnist Sidney Skolsky. The big change occurred however when Joseph M. Schenck introduced Monroe to Harry Cohn, the infamous head of Columbia Pictures, who was impressed by her aura and signed her up in March of 1948. It was Cohn who saw the sex vamp potential in Marilyn, urging her to re-style herself, dye her hair blonde and adopt a new kind of sassiness. Again though, despite a bit of buzz, her only film for Columbia was Ladies of the Chorus (1948), an early starring role which showed

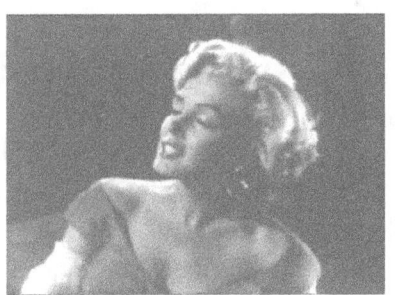

shades of her future promise but was not a hit.

There was another shift the following year when she met Johnny Hyde, president of the William Morris Agency. They entered an intimate relationship and he even asked for hand in marriage. Marilyn turned him down, but their professional partnership resulted in her getting a role in the late period Marx Brothers film, Love Happy, which was released in 1950. Given she was still very much in the embryonic phase of her career, and had to pay the bills, Monroe posed nude for some calendar shoots by Tom Kelley, released by John Baumgarth. These shots would come back to haunt her later and would become some of the most iconic Marilyn shots ever taken.

Still, her acting career was on the up. In the early fifties she made a series of films, though her parts were mostly small. She worked for John Huston in his seminal crime thriller The Asphalt Jungle (1950) and appeared in a run of successful Fox comedies, As Young As You Feel, Love Nest and Let's Make It Legal. Her popularity grew speedily and even the scandalous re-emergence of the nude pictures won her approval from her fans. She made the cover of Life Magazine in 1952 and began to attract serious attention in Hollywood.

Marilyn earned acclaim for her acting in Clash by Night and Don't Bother to Knock, proving that the acting lessons had paid off. While she was still playing off her sexy image in the comedic likes of Monkey Business, she proved she was also a serious artist. Unfortunately, she was gaining the reputation for being difficult, often being late on set and argumentative with directors. Still, none of this affected her popularity as she entered 1953, her most important year yet. She expanded her range as a sexy femme fatale in Niagara, which was possibly the best performance she had given up to that point. It led into one of her most lasting and iconic film roles, in Gentlemen Prefer Blondes, and she completed the year with How to Marry A Millionaire, alongside Betty Grable and Lauren Bacall. Again, it became a firm Monroe classic.

In this era Monroe was not only fighting for more pay (the studio had not altered her contract since the early days, meaning that for such a rising star she was being paid much less than other well known actresses) but against the shallow pin up roles that studio head Darryl F. Zanuck insisted she take. Marilyn wanted to expand her range but he was adamant that Monroe would not be a box office drawer in more dramatic parts.

Marilyn's personal life also began to change drastically. In January of 1954, the same month she entertained troops in Korea, she married baseball megastar Joe

DiMaggio. Once back home, she managed to wrangle a new deal with Fox; not only would she have a say in her upcoming projects, she also bagged herself a $100,000 bonus.

Though Monroe did not like the film itself, 1954's River of No Return was a smash hit and gave audiences the chance to see Monroe in a more earthy part. Her next monumental success came later that year with Billy Wilder's The Seven Year Itch, one of the most important and loved American films of the decade. It was another sexy pin up role, but the film itself had a deeper meaning, was hilarious, and resonated with audiences everywhere.

Monroe was at the height of her fame, but her movie success was coupled with personal troubles when she and DiMaggio divorced after only nine months. She set up her own production company and rebelled once more against Fox who were insisting on clichéd roles capitalising on her beauty and sex appeal. Monroe also famously relocated to Manhattan where she enlisted in Lee

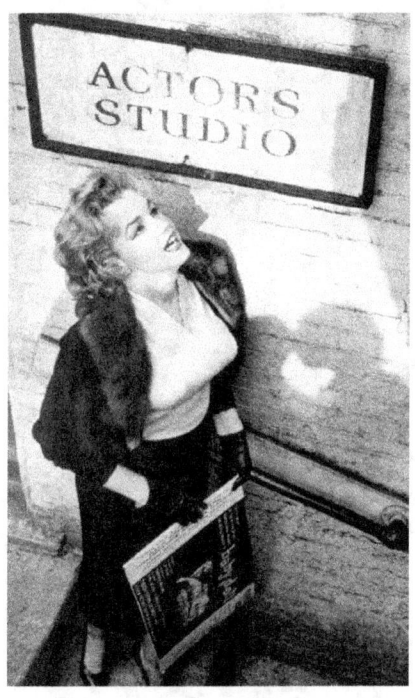

Straberg's Actor's Studio. Natasha Lytess, Monroe's acting coach, was speedily replaced by Lee's wife Paula, who Marilyn remained hugely dependant on for years. In truth, the Strasbergs adored Monroe, invited her into their lives and nurtured her talent when everybody else wanted to limit her to one type of role.

She then met the man who many claim was the true love of her life, the genius playwright Arthur Miller.

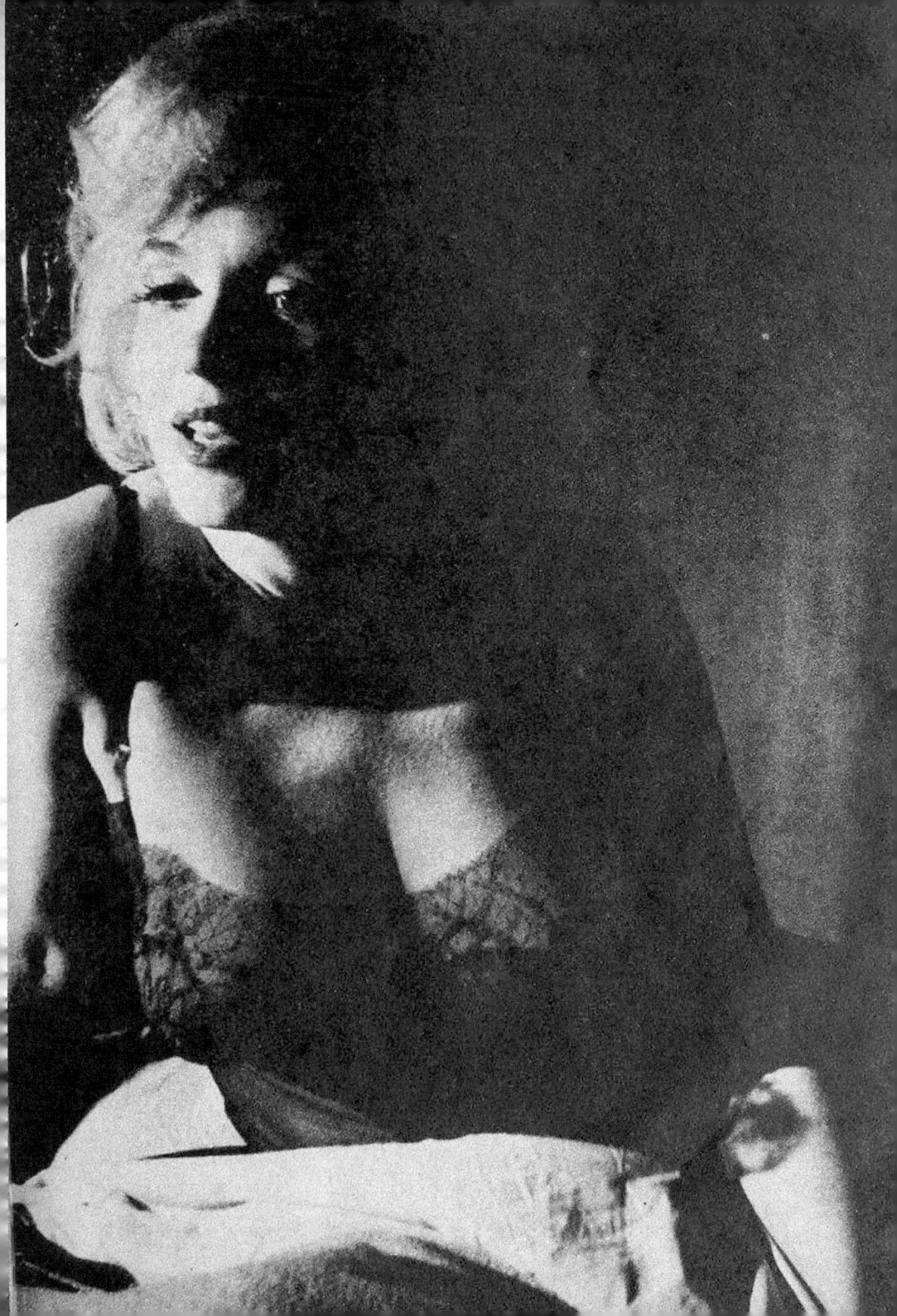

They remained a couple through Monroe's most iconic years to follow. Triumphantly, Marilyn won her case against 20th Century Fox and finally gained control of her own career. She garnered acclaim for her part in Bus Stop, which highlighted her dramatic skills, and in 1956, the year she married Miller, she worked with the World's Greatest Actor, Laruence Olivier, on The Prince and the Showgirl. Though her work and the film itself is appreciated

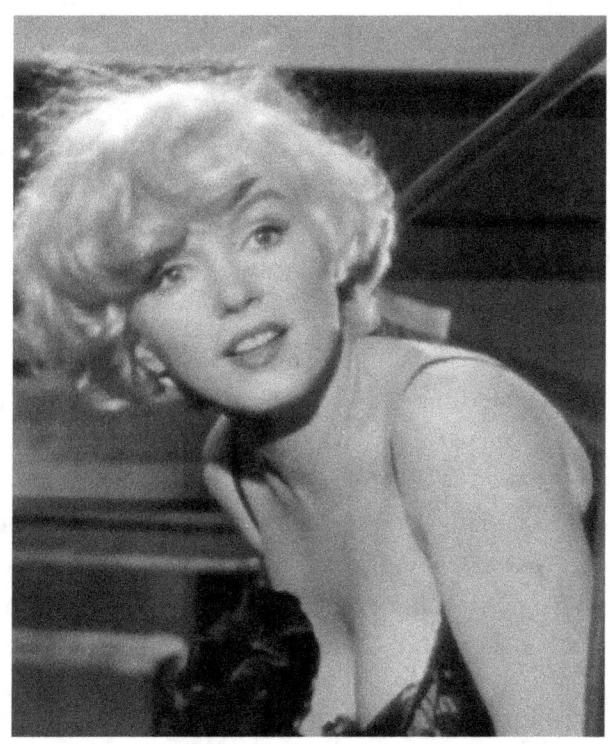

these days, it was a disappointment to many upon release and Monroe did not enjoy working with the patronising Olivier. It was on the set of Olivier's film that she began to rely on pills, and one could say this was the great turning point for her, when the demons which had plagued her for years began to overtake her. And the more successful and famous she was, the worse her problems became.

After the stressful making of The Prince and the Showgirl, she and Miller took a year and half long break to focus on their relationship. They tried to have children but Monroe suffered both a miscarriage and an ectopic pregnancy. She returned to work in July of 1958 to star in Some Like It Hot, the mega-successful comedy which earned her great acclaim and a Golden Globe for her performance. Though the making of the film was difficult and her relationship with director Billy Wilder strained to say the least, Some Like It Hot became one of her most loved pictures.

The turn of the sixties marked a drastic shift in Monroe's life and career. She shot Let's Make Love in late 59 with Yves Montand, but the film was not a success and was ill-received by critics. She was then directed by the great John Huston in 1961's The Misfits, written by Miller and co-starring Clark Gable. Though not a huge success at the time, it later became a cult film and today many see Monroe's performance in the film as her finest. After filming however, Miller and Monroe sadly divorced.

She spent much of the rest of 1961 out of the public eye, in and out of hospital for various reasons, including a bout of surgery and a four week stint with depression. Monroe also began making Something's Got to Give with Dean Martin, but it was never finished and the filming was wrought with difficulties, resulting in Fox suing Monroe for damages. Marilyn had more work mapped out but she didn't live to see any of these films come to fruition. She died on the night of August 4, between 8:30 and 10:30, of barbiturate poisoning.

Monroe's life has been examined countless times on TV, in books and magazine articles, been speculated and dissected for close to six decades. While many of the mysteries and complexities of her life and death cannot be solved or understood, the film work she left behind can at least be appreciated and admired, and it is through this that she remains immortal, forever dazzling and beautiful, but also sad. It is truly an extraordinary run of films, and Monroe's work in them should not be undervalued or taken for granted.

The following articles explore what I feel to be Monroe's finest film performances, in the likes of River of No Return and The Misfits...

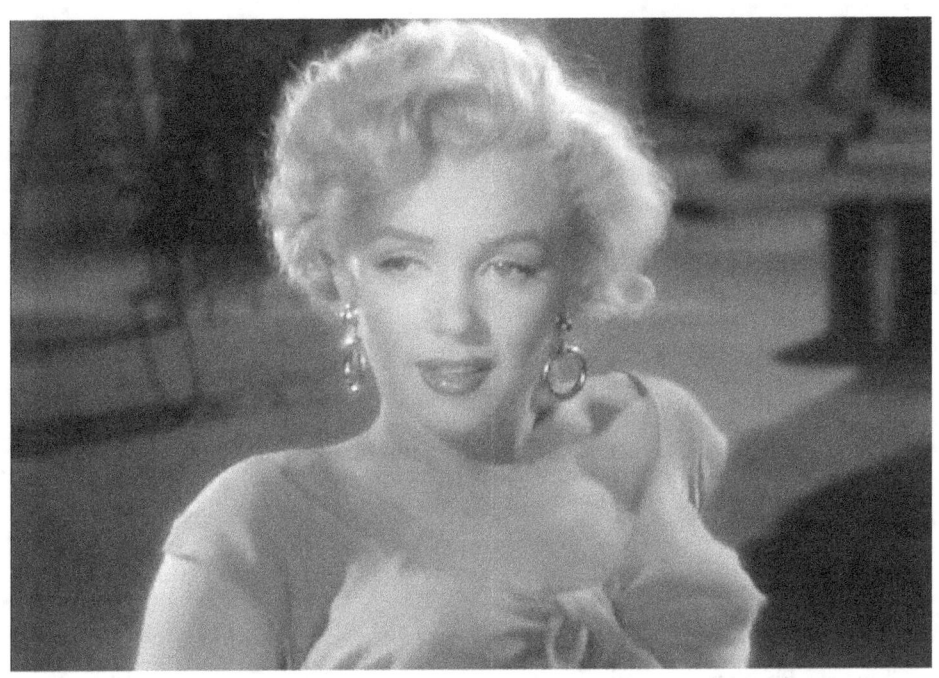

CLASSIC MONROE: NIAGRARA

Niagara may not be the most obvious choice when it comes to singling out key Marilyn performances, but in my view it is the first time she electrifies the viewer and becomes impossible not to watch and study. Of course she had been good before this, but Niagara and her performance in it hits you full on. This femme fatale role, far from any other part she ever played, still feels very modern and in fact comes across as a blueprint for all the wicked females that have come since in countless thrillers and dramas. Here, she sizzles and turns up the heat like no other.

The picture, released in 1953 and directed by the great Henry

Hathaway, concerns a young couple who arrive in Niagara Falls to find their booked holiday retreat is still occupied by a couple, ageing grouch Joseph Cotton and sexy Marilyn. From the get go the pair spell trouble, and the wide eyed young couple (played by Jean Peters and Max Showalter) find themselves dragged in to the kind of world they never knew existed.

The project itself began when Charles Brackett asked Walter Reisch to concoct a story about Niagara Falls, and Reisch, thinking outside the box, opted not for a romance but a murder story. Once he had the plot put together he began work on the script with Brackett and Richard L Breen. It was head honcho Darryl F Zanuck who decided on casting Monroe, only he surprised the film's writers with his idea on using her as, not the good girl, but the villainess. "My God!" recalled Reisch. "Here was the prettiest girl in the whole United States of America! But he insisted it was a great idea, so we finally did it. We didn't know whether she would like it, but she had no objection, whatsoever—on the contrary."

Monroe, already wanting a way out of predictable roles, jumped at the chance and gave the part her all. Casting the stunning young Marilyn was a touch of genius, but the real art here is in her film stealing performance. She radiates, she glows, but she also simmers and schemes in a way that makes her the ultimate femme fatale, irresistible but also a force of quiet destruction. It is, in my view, the guide on how to play a real femme fatale. Though there had been great female parts in film noirs before this, they were usually in moody black and white. The decision to film in colour not only separated it from other noir thrillers, it also brought out the magic of the location and the blinding glamour and beauty of Monroe herself. This is film magic, much of it down to the effervescent Marilyn.

The film was a hit at the time and has since become a classic. Though critics admired the picture, many doubted, for some strange reason, Marilyn's abilities. New York Times commended the final product, but wrote of Monroe: "For the producers are making full use of both the grandeur of the Falls and its adjacent areas as well as the grandeur that is Marilyn Monroe... Perhaps Miss Monroe is not the perfect actress at this point. But neither the director nor the gentlemen who handled the cameras appeared to be concerned with this. They have caught every possible curve both in the intimacy of the boudoir and in equally revealing tight dresses. And they have illustrated pretty concretely that she can be seductive - even when she walks. As has been noted, Niagara may not be the place to visit under these circumstances but the falls and Miss Monroe are something to see."

Variety also noted Hathaway's usage of Marilyn, writing "Niagara is a morbid, clichéd expedition into lust and murder. The atmosphere throughout is strained and taxes the nerves with a feeling of impending disaster. Focal point of all this is Marilyn Monroe, who's vacationing at the Falls with hubby Joseph Cotten... The camera lingers on Monroe's sensuous lips, roves over her slip-clad figure and accurately etches the outlines of her derrière as she weaves down a street to a rendezvous with her lover."

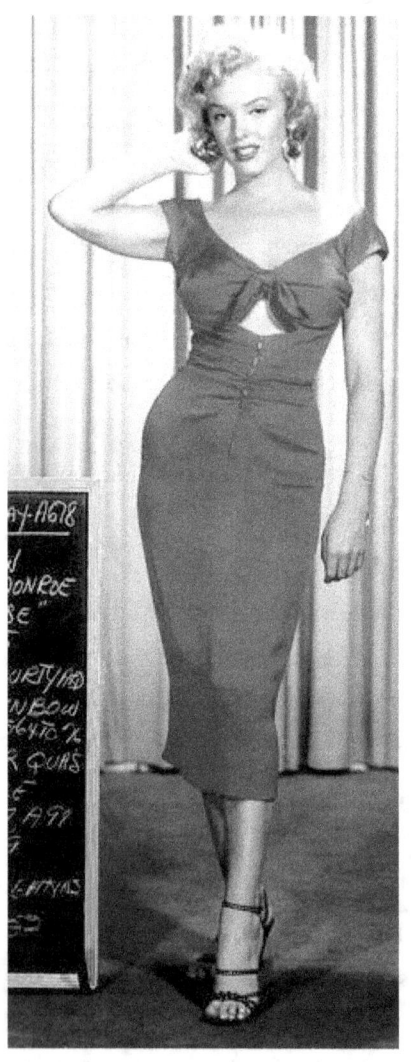

Niagara is now well known for THAT walk scene, the longest in film history as it was once reported. For me however, one of the key scenes here is less subtle, but highlights Marilyn's sexual magnetism and power over the camera. She is in bed, naked beneath the cover. Cotton comes back to the lodge and she quickly lies down and pretends to be asleep. When he gets to bed and turns away from her, she opens her eyes. It is in that look, half smirking, that Monroe's part can be defined. She turns away in the bed and goes to sleep, before the change into the next scene. For me, this pre-echoes what Monroe is about to do in the film but also illustrates how aware she was of what the camera could capture in her. For this scene alone, anyone doubting Marilyn's abilities will no doubt change their mind.

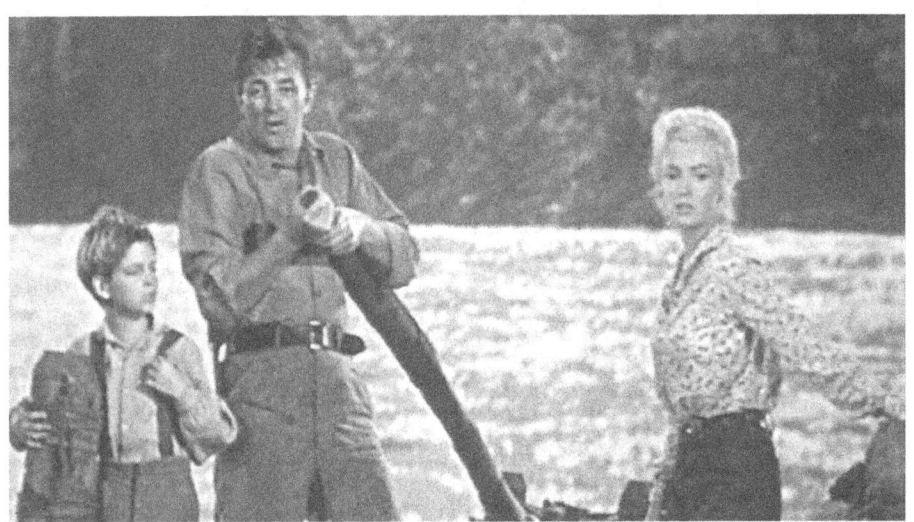

CLASSIC MONROE: RIVER OF NO RETURN

One of Marilyn's most underrated films is 1954's charming and genuinely engaging, River of No Return. Directed by Otto Preminger and with a script by Frank Fenton (from an original story by Louis Lantz), it's a visually beautiful, character-driven piece, a Western without the usual saloons, showdowns and gun fights of more familiar entries in the genre. Indeed,

River of No Return pulls the viewer in, not with non stop machismo action, but with the people who make their way through this most human and relatable of settings. The backdrop may be the lush mountains and rivers of 1870s North Western America, but the predicaments, hopes and dreams of the three protagonists makes it open to the viewer, whatever their time or setting may be.

The film stars Robert Mitchum as Matt Calder, a widower who we later learn has just come out of prison for shooting a man dead in an honour killing while protecting a friend.

Coming into a rag tag tent city frequented by rough and ready types, he finds his estranged son Mark (played by Tommy Rettig), who's developed a bond with the town's cabaret signer, the striking Kay (Monroe). Matt takes the boy away on horse back and the pair head out for a life in the wild. Meanwhile Kay hooks up with her swindling no-good boyfriend Harry (Rory Calhoun), and they too head down the river, meeting up with Matt and Mark at their cabin in the wilderness. Unfortunately, Harry turns Matt's own gun on him and takes off with his horse. Kay however, unable to leave the boy stranded in the country, where unarmed he and his father will fall victim to wild animals and Native Indians, stays with them. At first she struggles with the fact that her boyfriend is a cheap crook and would sell her down the river (no pun intended) at the drop of a hat, and has a somewhat jarring relationship with the no-nonsense Matt, who swears to act out revenge on Harry when he eventually tracks him down. However, as the film progresses and they make their journey down the river towards Council City, the bond between man, woman and child strengthens to the point that they become a kind of unexpected family, though she remains convinced that she and Harry will live happily ever after with the supposed fortune he has obtained. Will Matt find Harry, the man who did him wrong, and will Kay commit to a purer life away from the saloon bars?

From the moment it begins, River of No Return has you hooked. Preminger's assured, expertise direction is simple and straight forward, the kind of no-frills direction a Western needed in this golden era, especially one shot in glorious Cinescope. The film looks wonderful, with the stars and scenery alike captured splendidly by cinematographer Joseph LaShelle. It's aesthetically so impressive in fact that it's understandable why some critics at the time focused more on the backdrop, Monroe's undeniable

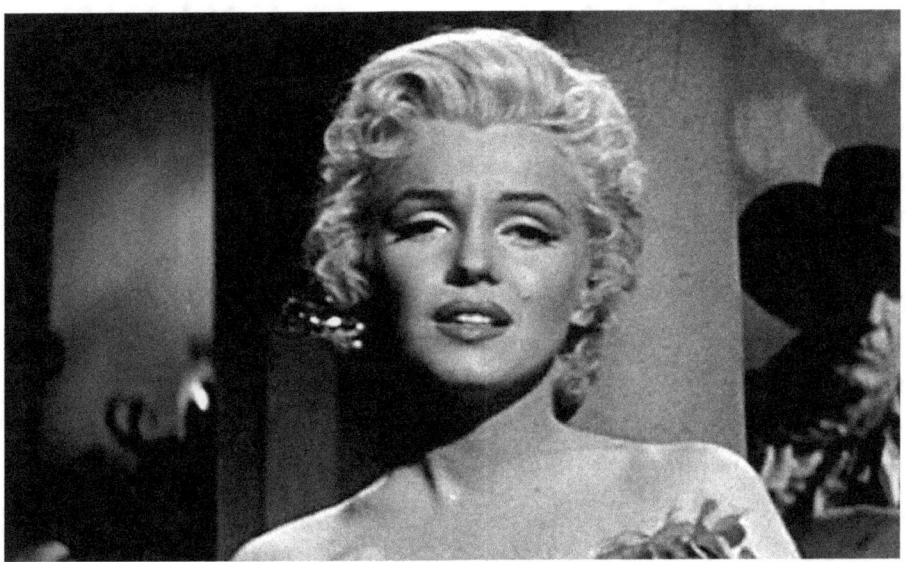

beauty and the rich colour than the story itself. But these reviewers were doing the film's content a disservice. Fenton's script is well paced, grounded in its own way, and features more than its fair share of memorable lines. It seems that in every scene, Mitchum utters a bit of dialogue so quotable that each witticism, quip and remark deserves classic status.

As handsomely shot it is, for me it was the performances, so carefully played out, that impressed the most. Mitchum is solid as ever, the strong male who can handle trouble but is also a gentleman. He is the firm leading man here, carrying us through this rootsy tale with his assured reliability. Audiences may be more used to seeing Mitchum in urban noir settings, but he is equally at home and effective in the rural outback.

Monroe too is dazzling. She is the epitome of glamour in the cabaret/dance hall scenes, bringing some colour and raw razzmatazz to the cheap, rowdy surroundings of the tent city. This is the kind of role many half-fans or modern day admirers of Marilyn will be more familiar with. But for me, the most interesting side to her performance in River of No Return is when she's in the mountains, the cabin, and fighting against the elements on the river. In her jeans, loose shirts and vest, her blonde hair free, she is every bit the country girl of the Wild West era. When she picks up the guitar and sings the boy a sweet song about the passing of the seasons, she takes you away on a cloud, beyond the movie she is in and to some glorious dream where Marilyn herself is still among us. But Monroe is adaptable to everything the film throws at her. In the famous scenes on the river, when they steer the raft through the treacherous, wild waters, we believe she is fully capable of making her way through the hardest, fastest waves. This not a cardboard performance, but a fully rounded one. Kay may be a saloon girl, a woman who performs for drunkards, but she is also a woman with a dream, a wide eyed girl with hopes of her own, but one who is not naive enough to think they could ever really come true in

the way she first pictured with her far from perfect lover. In the natural world, as sweet as she is to the boy and understanding of Matt's harsh ways, she comes into her own, existing in a reality she quite happily takes to, even if it could not be further away from the classy hotels and opera concerts she once fantasised of.

River of No Return was filmed partly on location in Calgary from June, 1953. Monroe came along with her acting coach, Natasha Lytess, who did not get along with Preminger. Otto tried to get her banned from the set, but Monroe put her foot down and said she would quit the film if her coach, a woman she relied on very much, were sent home. Darryl F. Zanuck could see where Preminger was coming from, but complied with Marilyn, because she was already such a star and guaranteed healthy box office. As a result, the relationship between Otto and Marilyn suffered. Preminger also suffered the side effects of Mitchum's heavy drinking habits and an injury

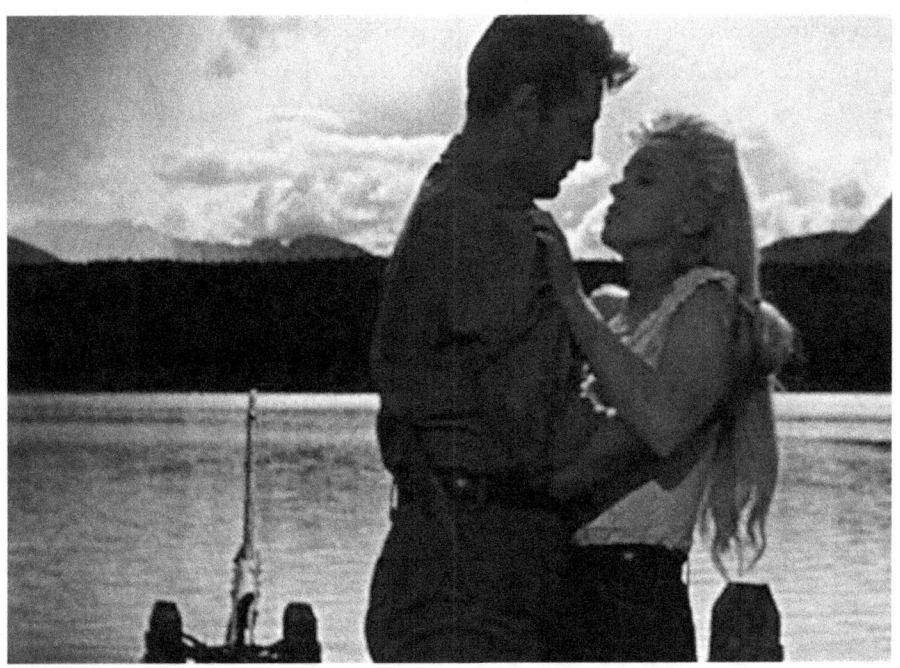

Marilyn suffered when slipping on the rocks on the river, where her boots were filled with water and she had to be rescued by Mitchum.

They returned to Los Angeles for the interior scenes in September of 1953, including close ups of Mitchum, Rettig and Monroe on the raft, against a screen which projected footage shot on the Salmon River, the famous River of No Return of the title in Idaho. Despite these considerable difficulties, and Monroe's dissatisfaction with the whole film, filming completed at the end of September.

It's hard to understand these days, but upon completion of the film it was deemed a mistake to have employed Preminger as director. When viewing the footage, producer Stanley Rubin felt Otto had failed to capture the vibe of the Old West, at least according to the usual Hollywood stereotypes. In my view, that is what separates River of No

Return from other Westerns of the period. It doesn't feel like any other, and in fact comes across as a more universal setting. We are spared the usual clichés and familiarities of the genre, and this is certainly down to the fact that the director was European.

Despite the lack of faith behind the scenes however, River of No Return was a box office hit and also received some positive notices, though as previously stated most people seemed to over emphasise the location and Monroe's appearance. The New York Times review, written by Bosley Crowther, sums up many a critic's view: "It is a toss-up whether the scenery or the adornment of Marilyn Monroe is the feature of greater attraction in River of No Return... The mountainous scenery is spectacular, but so, in her own way, is Miss Monroe. The patron's preference, if any, probably will depend upon which he's interested in. Certainly, scriptwriter Frank Fenton has done the best he could to arrange for a fairly equal balance of nature and Miss Monroe... And that should not be too lightly taken. For Director Otto Preminger has thrown all the grandeur and menace of these features upon the eye-filling CinemaScope screen. A sickening succession of rapids, churned into boiling foam, presents a display of nature's violence that cannot help but ping the patron's nerves. The raft tumbling through these rapids is quite a sight to see. And layouts of Rocky Mountain landscapes are handsome in colour, too. But Mr. Mitchum's and the audience's attention is directed to Miss Monroe through frequent and liberal posing of her in full and significant views."

Sadly, Marilyn later called the film the worst she had ever appeared in, though one feels she may have been corrupted by the tone of many of the reviews. When an interviewer brought it up during some TV coverage the year after its release, Marilyn smiled, cringed a little and boldly said, "Let's not talk about that!" One wonders whether time may have changed her view on the picture. Had

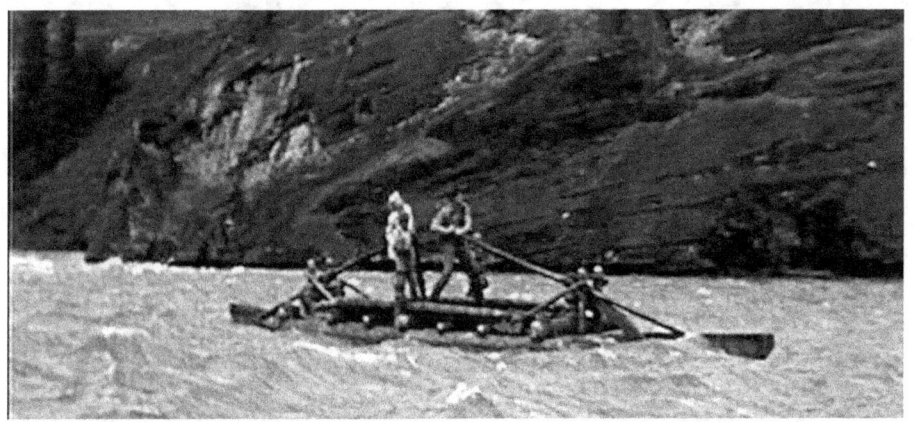

she maybe viewed it again further down the line (and had she lived of course), she may have seen all that was good about it, and how assured her performance was. Alas, it was not to be.

In the world of Marilyn, it's rarely picked out as one of her best and remains somewhat ignored. It has a better reputation now than it did before, yet reviewers still seem to be unconvinced by the characters and their relationships. Film 4 recently wrote, rather shallowly I might add, "The plot doesn't convince, but Monroe, at the peak of her career, is more than easy on the eye... Despite some pretty locations and occasional tension, there's little going on."

For me, River of No Return is one of Marilyn's finest pictures, not just for its story and how it's shot, but due to her performance. It has that air of melancholia which made all her work magic by it simply being her, but there is something special here. This is one of her best pieces of acting work, where she excels in every scene and seems to insert her all into every line of dialogue. It's a film which gives her plenty of space to explore facets of herself and her character, meaning they often overlap and create a poignancy which is very touching. This is a film that deserves more acclaim and it will hopefully get it in the years that follow.

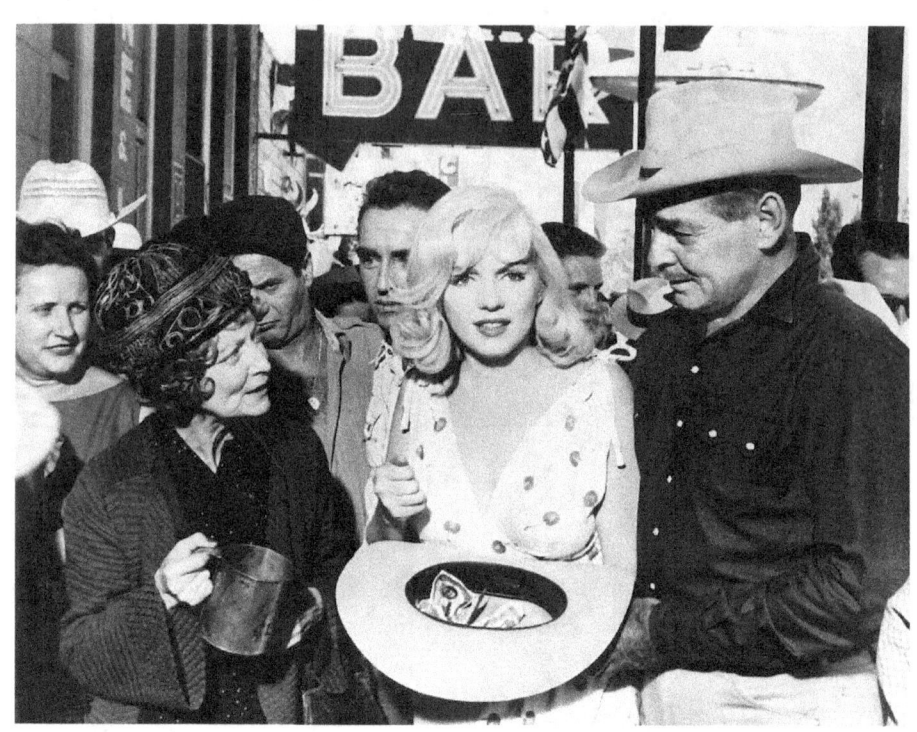

CLASSIC MONROE:
THE MISFITS (1961)

The Misfits is a film which is impossible to watch without thinking of the tragedies and events surrounding and following its filming and release. It remains, sixty years after it was completed, one of the saddest, most moving and haunting pictures of all time. Its melancholic eeriness is not just in the fact that it was the final film of both Marilyn Monroe and Clark Gable, but a whole host of things; its stark locations, the whirlwind of faces, John Huston's intimate direction, Arthur Miller's wonderful script and the committed, raw and electrifying performances within it. It's hard to truly define what makes The Misfits such a special movie, but all these factors and more go some way to doing so.

The Misfits script was written in the late fifties, when Miller was urged by Marilyn to write something for film in which she could take the starring role. When he did get round to it, the finished script bore little resemblance to anything Monroe had done before in her film career. In her previous films there had been hints of melancholia, but never before had a script captured the sad brilliance and tortured genius of what it was to be Marilyn Monroe. Monroe may have been shocked by what she read in her husband's screenplay - especially given he had so efficiently nailed her magnetism, appeal, insecurities and shortcomings - but she could not deny its brilliance.

Lest we forget, Miller was already an icon of the stage prior to The Misfits, with plays like All My Sons, The Crucible and Death of a Salesman to his name, all of which had redefined American theatre. But The Misfits was different. It would have been equally effective on the stage, but it was written for movie stars. Speaking years later, Miller himself said "I would not have written it except for Marilyn. I wrote it for her. It was the only time I did write anything for an actor and, had I not known her, I would not have begun such a thing. She had lost a child in early pregnancy, which really upset her a lot, so it was a kind of a gift. It was also the expression of a kind of belief in her as an actress."

John Huston, who had directed Monroe in her earlier years in The Asphalt Jungle, was hired to direct. Miller later said he felt Huston understood Marilyn, and saw her, perhaps, as a kind of mad genius. With Huston being very much his own man, he was not familiar with the Hollywood gossip surrounding Monroe and how difficult she was known to be on set. Once informed of this, he was still not put off and signed up with confidence that he was working with a genuinely brilliant script by one of the theatre's leading writer. Clark Gable was cast as Gay, while the troubled Montgomery Clift, Thelma Ritter and Eli Wallach were also added to the ensemble cast.

The story of the film concerns Roslyn Tabor (Monroe), a young woman who undergoes a speedy divorce from her estranged husband and seems to be spending a lot of time with lonely fellow-divorcee Isabelle (Thelma Ritter), who also happens to be her landlady. After the court hearing, the two women head to a bar where they bump into two interesting characters; one is Guido (Eli Wallach), a tow truck driver who they met earlier in the day; the other is Gay Langland, an ageing cowboy with a twinkle in his eye. After chatting, they agree to head out to Guido's country home, which he rarely sets foot in, given the fact he had lived there with his recently deceased wife and the place reminds him of his happy marriage. It's unfinished, is rough around the edges, but while Rosalyn stays there she begins to pull it round and give it a little of the woman's touch.

Expectedly perhaps, given his track record with women, Gay and Roslyn hook up and begin staying at Guido's house. Speedily, though it's never happened before, Gay falls in love with her and reveals intimate details about the family he left behind. Isabelle and Guido arrive, with the latter bringing up the idea of going out with Gay in the desert to capture some wild mustangs to raise some cash. They then run into Perce (Montgomery Clift), a wild and reckless rodeo performer who comes along for the ride, adding another face to this unlikely gang of outsiders. It becomes clear that all three men are head over heels in love with Roslyn, this woman of pure beauty who seems to have come out of nowhere to brighten their lives, even if she seems incapable of brightening her own. It all leads to a climax in the dessert, where the misfits are planning on capturing the wild horses. Roslyn cries for Gay to set them free, and that she will give him the 200 dollars if he does so. Offended, he refuses, while Guido says he'll cut the ropes if she leaves Gay for him. In the end, Gay sets

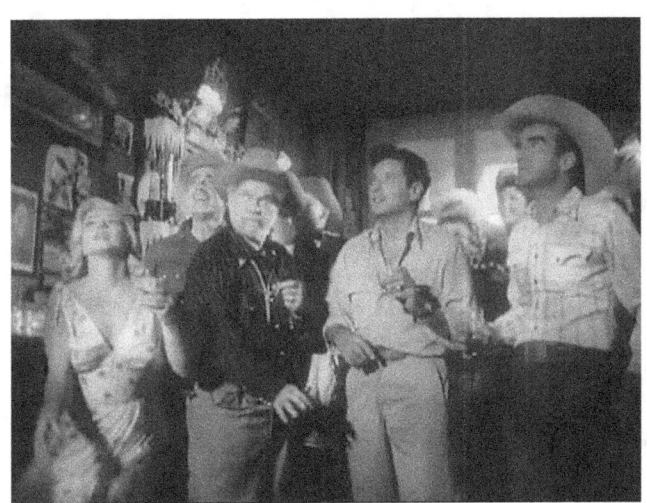

and crew. This caused some tension, as did Monroe's lateness and bizarre behaviour, not to mention the growing strain of her and Miller's relationship which crumbled as filming went on. Fittingly, Miller developed the screenplay as filming went on, tweaking and making changes.

them loose himself, on his own accord; quite simply, he "didn't want anyone making up his mind for him". The film ends with Gay and Roslyn driving into the desert following a glowing star in the night sky.

The Misfits was filmed in Northern Nevada in temperatures which exceeded 100 degrees. Though Monroe was at times difficult on set, Huston took it in his stride and remained professional, even when Monroe's takes entered the double figures. As usual, Monroe was accompanied at all times by Paula Strasberg, who in her black outfits unsettled certain members of the cast

Monroe was not the only one acting weirdly. Huston himself, a famous drinker and gambler, was often out all night at casinos where he would bet thousands of dollars and drink into the wee hours. Eli Wallach got a glimpse into how Huston functioned with his drinking. During a scene with Eli portraying Guido drunk, Huston told him he was overplaying, then proceeded to inform Wallach that the previous day was the most drunk he'd ever been. Wallach told Huston that he seemed sober, and Huston agreed, giving him the key

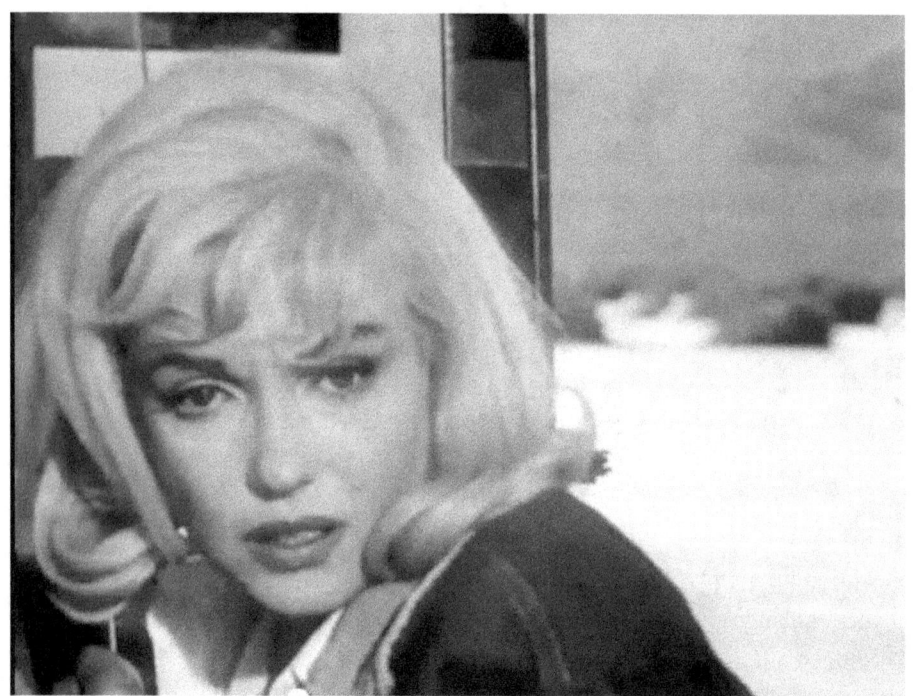

bit of direction on how to perform the scene - as well as a glimpse into how Huston chose to live his life. Gable was heard to comment at one point that he and Huston were the same age, and if he were to carry on living the way he did he'd be dead in a few years. Ironically, Gable died shortly after filming The Misfits, whereas Huston lived another thirty or so years.

Montgomery Clift was also troubled during the shoot, and was at the start of a slow decline which resulted in his premature death in 1966. He had recently suffered a serious car crash and had become addicted to alcohol and painkillers. Monroe herself was already hooked on medication at this point, and later said that Clift was the only person she'd met who was in worse shape than she was.

Monroe herself was drinking heavily after work, and combining this massive alcohol intake with prescription drugs was her downfall. With the upset of her break up from Miller, and the substances she was letting in her body, Monroe was put into hospital for exhaustion and depression. Huston had to halt filming in August while Marilyn recuperated. Filming eventually wrapped up in November of 1960, and Gable was to die only 12 days later.

Despite the various issues, the whole cast are fabulous, and it may even be due to their real life demons that the film is as poignant as it is. Clift gives a wonderfully raw and moving performance, channelling the method style into a ragged and often painful-to-watch depiction of a lost soul just getting used to life as an outlaw of society. Eli Wallach gives a tremendous performance as Guido, the decent man utterly besotted by Roslyn and missing his dead wife, a man too aware that he's at a dead end. Gable too, is magnificent, for me giving the best performance of his career, which makes it al the more poetic that it was his final bow. His lived in face comes out the crisp black and white and reminds you of the sheer size of his legacy. Gable also did his own stunts during the shoot, which concerned those close to him. But he was adamant, especially during the final mustang scene, that he should be the man doing the physical work so vital to the film's conclusion. In retrospect, many involved in the filming believe the stunts contributed to his subsequent heart attack.

As great as the rest of the cast are though, the film belongs to Marilyn, who is utterly mesmerising as the sweet but troubled Roslyn. It is clear she put a lot of thought (and Strasberg's advice) into every scene, every line of dialogue, every gesture for that matter, but there is a fifth element to the performance which transcends anything she is doing as an actress. And as wonderful as her work is, it's in the depths of Marilyn that her performance enters a whole different league. She is haunted, sad, tormented even, and the weight of her life is there behind her empty eyes. Her almost otherworldliness gives the role and the whole film a strange spookiness, but the tragedy is beyond poignant, beyond moving, and something close to dark magic.

She has a number of scenes in The Misfits which are among the best of her all too short career. One sequence in particular is perhaps the most chilling of her filmography; it comes after the gathered friends have been drinking and dancing in Guido's house, and Marilyn goes outside to dance on the grass, under the trees in the darkness of the night. The smiles fade from their faces and they see something other than the fun, sweet, beautiful girl from earlier in the day. They see her for what she is, a woman as lost as they are. It's a beautiful scene, but also suffocating in its hopeless darkness. Another stand out is when Clift first meets the band of misfits and speaks to Gable who is at the wheel of the car. He is leaning into the car, and Marilyn is between the two men observing their interaction. There is something in her eyes, a combination of wonderment and weariness, like a tired child, which elevates the whole scene, even though she doesn't utter a single word throughout. This is film acting on a whole other level. Undoubtedly, Roslyn is the deepest, saddest character Marilyn ever played, and it was a part written by a man who not only knew her well, but also loved her dearly. It is undoubtedly the finest performance she ever gave on film.

The film was released on the date of Gable's 60th birthday in 1961, and though he was dead Monroe and Clift did go to the premiere. Marilyn herself said she hated both the film and her performance, and held a grudge against Miller for exposing her so nakedly - emotionally that is - in his script. But it is obvious that her reaction was so because she knew Miller had gotten to the root of her. Marilyn was Roslyn, the beautiful but sad girl who every man loved, but who couldn't love herself. And he even includes the line he uttered to her when they both first met in the mid fifties - "I think you're the saddest girl I've ever seen." Art imitating life indeed. He'd delivered her a valentine; not the one she had hoped for perhaps, but the most real and sincere one possible.

Critics at the time were confused by the film; it was a film set in the West without Western themes; it starred Clark Gable but was far from being a typical Gable picture; and it had Marilyn Monroe at its centre, yet her character could not have been further from the ones she'd played before. As a result, this un-commercial picture, which Miller insisted put art before views of a profit, kind of slipped through the cracks. It was highly publicized at the time, left some audiences and critics cold, and only later, once people could see it from a distance, did it become a classic.

Some reviewers however appreciated the poetry of the piece, and also the fact that reality and fiction were often blurred indeed. The Village Voice wrote, "Marilyn Monroe, the Saint of the Nevada desert... She haunts you, you'll not forget her... It is MM that tells the truth in the movie, who accuses, judges, reveals. And it is MM who runs into the middle of the desert and in her helplessness shouts: "You are all dead, you are all dead!"—in the most powerful image of the film—and one doesn't know if she is saying those words to Gable and Wallach or to the whole loveless world... There is so much truth in her little details, in her reactions to cruelty, to false manliness, nature, life, death, that she is overpowering, one of the most tragic and contemporary characters of modern cinema."

In the UK, the Observer applauded the film, and they too were aware that the lines between Marilyn and Rosalyn were blurred. They wrote: "Occasionally a film arrives which gives the cinema a new dimension. Films like Battleship Potemkin, Citizen Kane, Bicycle Thieves, and

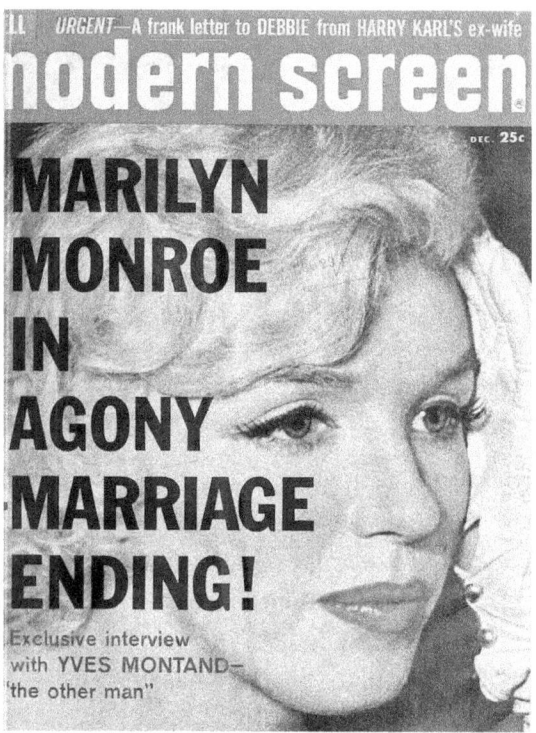

Hiroshima Mon Amour, marked a turning point in the cinema, influencing directors, actors, and audiences. It is not going too far to say that The Misfits is in this class. The individual performances are so good that with a thrill of recognition one sees what acting in the cinema can achieve. Clark Gable's performance is as casually professional as ever, and yet he brings to the ageing cowboy an intensity of feeling one never suspected he possessed. Miller's heroine is so obviously based on his former wife – one half expects the cast to blurt out Marilyn for Rosslyn every so often – that her performance is difficult to judge. Yet if she is merely playing herself she does it remarkably well."

Given its lack of story, and focus on character, other critics were confused, if not lost. The New York Times said of the characters that "They are scatterbrained, whimsical, lonely and, in the case of the character of Miss Monroe, inclined to adore all living creatures and have a quivering revulsion to pain. They are amusing people to be with, for a little while, anyhow. But they are shallow and inconsequential, and that is the dang-busted trouble with this film. Right at the start, Arthur Miller, who wrote the original script, drops a hint on what is coming and the line that the film is going to take. "Cowboys,"

38

he has a jolly woman, played by Thelma Ritter, say, "are the last real men in the world, but they're as reliable as jackrabbits." And that's it. Everyone in this film is unreliable, wild, slightly kookie."

And they added, as if watching a totally different film to the one we all know, "Miss Monroe—well, she is completely blank and unfathomable as a new divorcée who shed her husband because 'you could touch him but he wasn't there.' Unfortunately for the film's structure, everything turns upon her—the congregation of the fellows, like a pack of dogs, the build up of cross-purposed courtships and the sentimental back flip at the end. But there is really not much about her that is very exciting or interesting."

I do believe the main problem was that critics mistook Monroe's weariness for blankness. That was the point. She is a lost soul, stuck in a blizzard of activity, faces, whiskey glasses and goings on, yet she can't figure out who she is or where she belongs. One may argue that in going with Gay at the end she achieves a kind of happy ending, but then there's the fact they are heading nowhere in particular, and there is no place, as of yet, that they can call their home. There is no "the end" to The Misfits and that's what makes it brilliant.

These days though, people seem to get what Monroe is doing, whether she truly meant to do it or not. The Independent wrote in 2015, "Against the odds, she gives an extraordinary performance. It's an artless one that at times seems phoney, but what she does convey in uncanny and febrile fashion is her character's power of empathy, whether it is her sympathy for the cowboys (Clark Gable and Montgomery Clift) out of kilter with a modern, wages-based world, or for the wild mustangs they plan to kill."

The film won Marilyn a Golden Globe for World Film Favourite, a gong she would pick up only months before her death, and is now seen as not only one of Monroe's finest pictures, but one of the greatest in the history of American cinema.

FELLINI'S CITY OF WOMEN

AN ESSAY ON FEDERICO FELLINI'S UNDERRATED 1980 SURREAL MASTERPIECE

City of Women, the first of Federico Fellini's final five films, seems to divide long term admirers of the maestro. Some see it as a film which begins well, very well in fact, but descends into repetition about half way through. Others, while not claiming it to be Federico's finest film, or for that matter even among the best, admire it for the filmmaking feat it truly is, a typically dazzling Fellini dream, with the great man's imagination switched to eleven. Personally, I fall into the minority camp that sees City of Women as one of Fellini's true masterpieces. Not only is it possibly his most enjoyable picture, it is also one of his most direct, which leads to serious thought about the themes which come to the fore throughout.

On a basic level, this is another one of his fantastical descents into the subconscious, a surreal odyssey, which like both La Dolce Vita and 8 1/2, defies the usual logic associated with the modern narrative film and takes our lead character, once again Marcello Mastroianni, on an epic journey that is both an education and an enlightenment for him and the viewer. Beneath this well orchestrated, head spinning and dazzling surface is a film whose aims have been interpreted and unfortunately misinterpreted down the years. It is, we can all agree, a film about women and feminism, but what people *have* argued about is on which side Fellini stood; was he for or against it?

The birth of City of Women was not as simple as just Fellini settling down

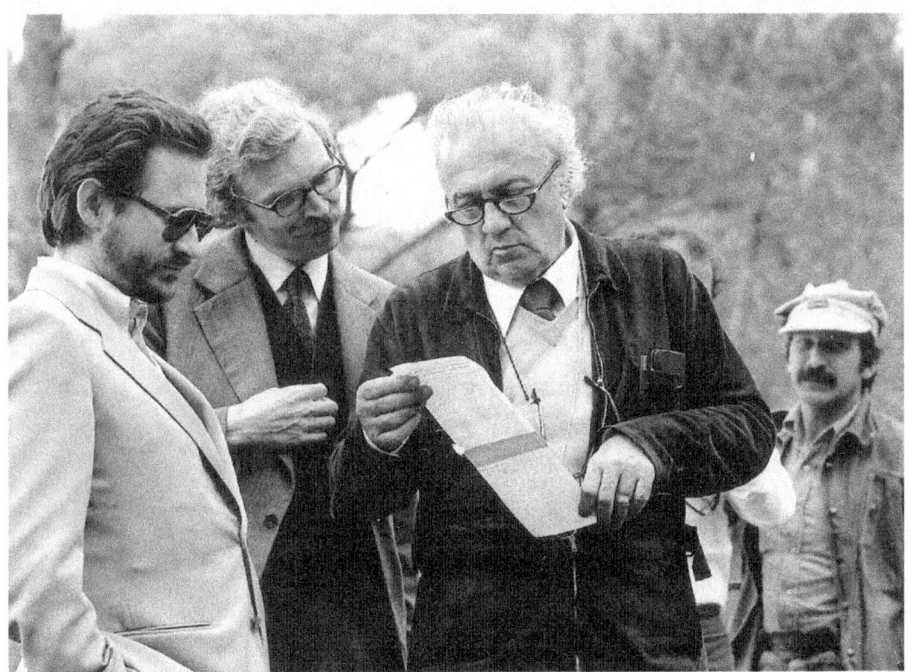

to make a movie about women. He originally wanted to write and direct a film about death, but producers steered him away from such an uncommercial subject. Fellini lifted some of the themes from his proposed projects and put them into the screenplay for City of Women, which he co-wrote with Bernardino Zapponi and Brunello Rondi. City of Women would be Fellini's unashamed exploration of the fairer sex, firstly as a species objectified by the male, and secondly as a gender who he believed to be superior. While making the picture Fellini made his views clear on women, when he was quoted as saying "I have the feeling all my films are about women. I am totally at their mercy; they are the only people I feel really at ease with. They represent the myth, mystery, diversity, fascination, the thirst for knowledge and the search for one's own identity. Women are everything. Going to the cinema is like returning to the womb. You sit there and meditate in the darkness, waiting for life to appear on the screen."

For Fellini, City of Women was more than a chance to make a film simply about women, but one which placed the male and the female in the centre of the feminist ideal. Friends say Fellini saw feminism as a caricature of an important belief system, rather than a serious manifesto, feeling it had gone down the wrong track and perhaps that the aggressive side of early feminism would only detract from the aim of the movement. He makes this clear in the film, though he does not completely damn it.

That said, he did not go running in with this theme in his head. "I could even say," he said, "that it is not I who choose a theme but the theme that chooses me, and then the film immediately takes shape and acquires images and feelings. In the end I come to the conclusion that I am enormously ignorant."

In the film, Marcello plays Snaporaz, a man in his fifties who wakes up while on a long train journey. He raises his head and has an instant attraction for the lady opposite him (played by Bernice Stegers) who he follows to the bathroom and attempts to have sex with. She gives him a passionate kiss but abruptly announces she is leaving the train. Speedily she hops off, heading not off the platform but towards a wooded area. Snaporez, debating mentally his next move, finally decides to follow the mysterious but sexy woman. Despite her brisk pace and increasingly mocking tone, he continues in his foolish pursuit. After she pushes him against a tree and convinces him to close his eyes for a big kiss, she disappears and Snaporez is left alone and lost in the thick wood.

Eventually he stumbles across a building and heads inside. The place is crammed full of activity, all of it female and chaotic. Snaporez finds himself in the thick of a feminist convention, something of a nightmare for an old fashioned sexist, but he tries to see things their way despite their full on aggression.

When the women begin to turn on him, he is led away into a lift by the kind and beautiful Donatella (played by Donatella Damiani). Bizarrely, she takes him to a skating rink and convinces him to put on a pair of skates. Again, the room is invaded by dozens of women skating round, eventually resulting in him taking a tumble down a staircase. In the basement he meets a larger woman who is seeing to the hotel's furnace, but promises to take him to the train station after she has washed. Mounting the back of her motorcycle, Snaporez and the lady breeze through the country side. But his adventure is not over yet. The woman insists they stop to see to some seeds in a greenhouse and they head inside, where she reveals a breast, tells him to feel its firmness and attempts to have sex with him, after which she is punished by her scrawny, aggressive mother. Snaporez is then escorted to a car where a group of girls who he hopes will take him to the station. He winds up in the middle of a convoy of female gangs and upon escaping

their sinister presence he winds up being taken in by Dr Katzone, an ageing lothario who resides in an

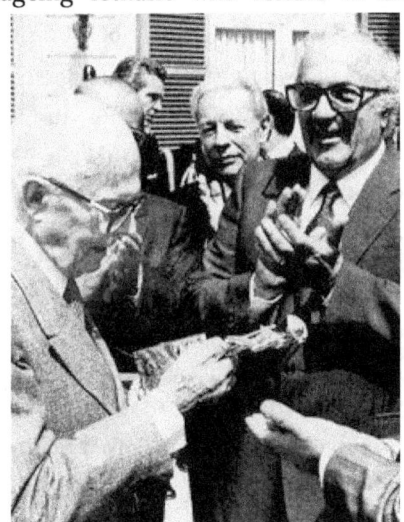

eccentric mansion, the corridors of which are decorated with surreal artworks dedicated to each of his many conquests. Later that night a party is hosted in honour of his 10, 000th sexual partner, and the lion haired doctor blows out all his candles in a rush of energy, even pissing on the highest circle of flames to extinguish them.

Snaporez's journey continues. At the party he encounters his wife, who announces she is leaving him, and is led to a bedroom by the kind and now scantily clad Donatella, who tucks him up in bed in an oversized night shirt. In an Alice in Wonderland-like turn of events, Snaporez winds up going under the bed and heading down a tunnel which leads to a surreal fun fair. He slides down a huge helter skelter, where actors recreate the women he adored as a child, as if to recount his sexual history. After this he is presented to a strange court that judges him for his machismo, who eventually set him free by directing him towards a huge ladder. While climbing up he breaks his glasses, the only thing left from the real world. It leads to a boxing ring, inside which sits a hot air balloon which is in the shape of Donatella herself. As he flies away to an apparent freedom, the real Donatella, who has offered him so many pleasant escapes throughout his adventure, shoots holes in the balloon, which begins to collapse. As he falls to what will surely be his death, Snaporez wakes up to find he is back on the train in the carriage. Seated before him is his wife, and coming into the carriage is the lady from the start of the film, who smiles knowingly. Other women from the supposed dream are also present, and, confused, Snaporez kneels down and picks up his glasses to see they are broken. The unusual atmosphere, the unsettling smirks from those around him and his broken spectacles suggest the dream may have been anything but a dream. As the train zooms speedily into a tunnel, the film comes to a close.

One's first thought is how City of Women could be Federico's own Alice in Wonderland, but from an adult male point of view. Snaporez, a veteran of love's harsh battlefield (or should that be lust), is paradoxically in both his own personal heaven and his purgatory. On the one hand he is surrounded by women throughout, some of them very attractive; however, they are all out for his blood, and these young, free, liberated, radical women see Snaporez in his old fashioned sexism as the enemy, anything but the Latin lover he may have been twenty years earlier. The ageing, tired lothario is a dinosaur in the face of their advancements, though he doesn't seem to learn from or absorb their ideas. At one point, when coming across three smiling women in relief, he comments on the aggression of feminism, perhaps unmasking Fellini's personal feelings about the movement's misdirection. But Snaporez is anything but an alter ego of Fellini, especially in his egotistical sexism. Fellini stated that he exaggerated certain aspects of feminism as if it were being viewed through the eyes of a man who not only couldn't understand it, but didn't really wish to, being so stuck to his antiquated views on women and their place in society. Snaporez, quite simply, typifies the outdated Italian male, the heartless ladies' man who objectifies the female and sees her as a play thing, clearly a man looking for trouble in the city of women.

Fellini saw Snaporez as a "little red riding hood wandering about in the forest." And though he surely knew the film was bound to be dissected and picked to pieces by modern thinkers, he wanted it to be a purely cinematic experience, another filmic dream, the kind he excelled at delivering to the public. "As the film is a dream it uses the symbolic language of dreams. I would like people to see it without trying to understand it, as there is nothing to be understood," he added. "I hate that contemporary sickness which manifests itself in a desperate need for an ideology. Everything has to be tried in a court of reason which analyses, diagnoses, and orders treatment for the unintelligible."

If taken as a film, a piece of dream like entertainment defying explanation, City of Women is enormously enjoyable. It is an odyssey, a film which never lets up and keeps on moving forward, though never becoming tiresome or tiring as it does so. Going form one exotic, lavish set piece to another, it is Fellini extravagance at its best, where one can see where the budget went and that not a penny was wasted. The convention sequences are spellbinding, magnificently handled by the master and staged wonderfully. The home of the womanising doctor, himself an example of the mad lover who yearns for all females to be submissive and highly sexualised, is a cave of wonders, hiding another surprise around each corner. It is Snaporez's only respite from the onslaught of the females, with Katzone being a safe face amidst the chaos. Katzone is also part of a dying breed, outlawed by the women who are out to demolish his home and put an end to his decades of shameless womanising. Yet even in the safety of Katzone's home he is attacked by his wife, a character Fellini referred to as a parody of the "pain in the ass housewife".

Another key character is Donatella, played by the gorgeous Donatella Damiani, a woman Fellini first saw on a picture showing only her face. He was transfixed by her features, her "sightless eyes", and thought she looked like some mythical woman from a tarot card. Only when

meeting her did Fellini see her unusually large breasts, especially for her slender frame. Federico was smitten, seeing her as a muse, so Donatella became an even more vital character in the film; a mother, a siren, a saviour, the approachable and kindly everywoman in the midst of this mad dream, and in one scene, clad in a glittery bikini, every man's sexual dream. "Although she is practically nude throughout the film," Fellini said, "she is never obscene. She is a kind of elfin or sprite like figure." Damiani is beautiful, of that there is no doubt, though in her versatility in the eyes of Snaporez she is never an object. Donatella may be one of the most striking women to ever have appeared on screen, but Fellini steers clear of making her a cliché.

Anyone looking to get offended by Fellini's supposed view of women and sexism, not to mention the nudity and sexual material in the film, should remember that not only is this a dream, it a dream of Snaporez, not Fellini. Snaporez does not understand women, meaning of course that he will not understand feminism either. Women are a mystery to him, explaining why when he does reach the boxing ring it is empty. Women are not opponents to him because they remain an enigma; and they, needless to say, remain mightier than he, above his simple minded objectifications. Yet with all this said, Fellini discouraged such speculations. It was, in his mind, simply about film as a magical experience, and City of Women certainly lives up to that ideal.

At the centre of this insanely enjoyable adventure is a marvellous performance from Mastroianni, once again perfecting his role as Fellini's journeyman, his involved but simultaneously disconnected male amidst the spinning tornado of wonderment, unable to make sense of the dream but happily (and sometimes unhappily) experiencing it for what it is, taking the rough with the smooth.

While on set in 1979, Marcello spoke to Corriere della sera about his part in the film: "What are you shooting tomorrow they always ask me. The fact is I haven't a clue. I don't even bother asking myself these days. I have gotten to the point where I'm simply enjoying myself. The psychological make up of this character is the same as in the other roles I have played for him (Fellini). Sometimes I even forget I am an actor; what I've become is a blend of myself and this character. What's important... is that it is a surrealistic journey. We have a man immersed in the adventure of re-encountering all the women who were most nutritious to him in the course of his life. Yes, nutritious is the very word."

For Marcello, the ageing ladies' man who had enjoyed romances with Catherine Duneuve, Faye Dunaway and Ursula Andress, a man who represented the old fashioned Italian no-nonsense viewpoint, of mid twentieth century masculinity, City of Women may have felt a little like looking in a mirror. The part called

47

for self reflection, of that there is no doubt. In the same interview he spoke of the fact that for him and Federico to understand modern women they would have to be twenty again. He says he fears that modern young men may be dissatisfied with their relationships, what he refers to as "conflicts with modern women". Though no Snaporez, Marcello was certainly an old fashioned man feeling somewhat bewildered in the face of this female revolution. In the film his character makes a valid point however. Repeating what one of the feminists said - "a scoundrel never changes" - quietly to himself while cleaning his spectacles, he asks himself, without expecting an answer, "but change into what?" Indeed, it's as if Marcello, and Fellini essentially, are accepting of these ideas, but wonder, quite validly, where they might be leading to. Castrated by the modern world, Snaporez/Marcello becomes de-masculinised, a man built on his libido forced to question his very existence as the alpha male in a world which sees him as a hopeless relic.

Yet Marcello defended the film's views on feminism, a movement he clearly accepted as a force for good. "There's been a lot of talk about a possible feminist reaction," Marcello added. "The fact is, the feminists in the film aren't put into a bad light at all. If anything, you can say that Federico views them through the eyes of someone his age. There is no judgement involved. And from time to time, Snaporez - me that is - observes all this, is touched and moved to feelings of great tenderness."

One hopes that Snaporez understands women better after his dream, and ideally might change his views on the fairer sex. Fellini himself explained Snaporez's understanding of himself through his subconscious: "In the end of City of Women the protagonist consciously accepts the fact that he is dreaming. Waking up in the train, and deciding to go back to sleep because reality is beginning to become upsetting again (he sees his wife in the seat previously occupied by the feminist, the feminist has become a sort of courtesan, the two terrorist sou- brettes turn out to be student girls), he accepts to go back into the tunnel with the knowledge that he now has made a contact with his inner, profound, mythical being. This time he will dream because he is deciding to dream. It will be a vigilant dream, full of attention for the profound, a witnessing dream. He goes back consciously into the dream in order to have a more lucid contact with himself."

But as Marcello himself stated in the interview, City of Women's philosophising is secondary to the very idea of it as a cinematic experience, an epic of the mind which, considering its existence in the subconscious, makes anything and everything, no matter how seemingly far fetched, perfectly acceptable. And like in La Dolce Vita, it is Marcello's controlled performance, his lack of over the top reactions and his measured, straight faced bewilderment, but also his dry acceptance of whatever comes in his path, which makes the film a perfect example of pure surrealism at its best. Abandoned, liberated and highly imaginative, it is for me the most underrated of Fellini's films, and arguably, though I may be on my own here, his finest achievement.

City of Women received some good reviews, but didn't set the world alight or garner the kind of acclaim it so rightly deserved. Roger Ebert, who so loved Fellini and Mastroianni's other work, felt it was seriously flawed, and found it hard to understand Fellini's view of women, who once had been important in his films as symbols but now had to be dealt with as human beings. Ebert wrote, "City of Women does nothing original or very challenging with this material. Although it pretends to be Fellini's film about feminism, it reveals no great understanding of the subject; Fellini basically sees feminists as shrill harems of whip-wielding harridans, forever dangling the carrot of sex just out of reach of his suffering hero. Fellini has rarely been able to discover human beings hidden inside his female characters, and it's a little late for him to start blaming that on the women's liberation movement. Is City of Women worth seeing? Yes, probably, even though it is not a successful movie and certainly not up to Fellini's best work. It's worth seeing because it's a bedazzling collection of images, because at times it's a graceful and fluid celebration of pure filmmaking skill, and because Fellini can certainly make a bad film but cannot quite make a boring one."

The New York Times, who saw City of Women as such a counterpart to 8 1/2 that it should be called 18 (given it was Fellini's 18th picture, including half entries for anthology instalments), found it a riveting spectacle: "Though the film is overlong, even for a Fellini aficionado, it is spellbinding, a dazzling visual display that is part burlesque, part satire, part Folies-Bergeres and all cinema. To interpret City of Women as antifeminist would

be, I think, to underrate the complexity of the man whose vision this is. Mr. Fellini obviously adores women as much as he adores making movies, especially movies that find substance in gaudy artifice..."

Of Marcello's controlled efforts, they wrote, "Mr. Mastroianni has never been better than he is here as the now well-seasoned Fellini surrogate figure. It's a supremely accomplished performance, modest and grand, broadly comic at times, even touching in its details. One special highlight: Mr. Mastroianni's doing a brief, elegiacal, Fred Astaire turn to the music of 'Let's Face the Music and Dance.' There is, though, no other single image in the film that equals the sight of Mr. Mastroianni's Snaporaz as he creeps under a bed, in pursuit of some new mystery, with a small hole in his left sock. It's at this moment that he finally surrenders his dignity. Forever."

Some modern reviewers, perhaps misunderstanding the main protagonist and mistaking him for a direct Fellini alter ego, have criticised its supposed sexism. The Quietus damned it as "Vulgar, Vampish and Vacuous. Fellini delves into the dark and obscure recesses of his psyche in search of his true self and turns up tumescent amid a carnival-esque cast of female beauties, hags, housewives, rampantly militant lesbians and a miniscule birdlike celebrity named Mrs. Small who has found inner sanctum through marriage to six docile husbands. Never let it be said that Federico Fellini was a crusading feminist, a beacon of hope for mis-represented females across the world. He wasn't. City of Women does nothing to alter this assessment."

Just as critics would misinterpret a film like Woody Allen's Stardust Memories as a direct attack on his fan base, naysayers too have targeted City of Women in their PC crusade as an outdated view of feminism through the eyes of a Jurassic creature. If they could perhaps see past the idea of it being autobiographical, rather than multi faceted and all encompassing, then they might enjoy it for the extravagant pleasure it truly is. This is a statement on women from various viewpoints, though it is vital to remember that Snaporez is not Fellini as 8 1/2s Guido surely was. Though City of Women will never be as praised as Fellini's more iconic work, one could argue it flows more smoothly than 8 1/2 and La Dolce Vita, feels more complete and focused, and also provides the viewer with more food for thought. One cannot undermine the brilliance of Marcello and Federico's earlier classics together, of course, but it must be said that City of Women, in all its glorious splendour, startling visuals, stunning set pieces and towering entertainment value, deserves to be up there with the great man's most appreciated work.

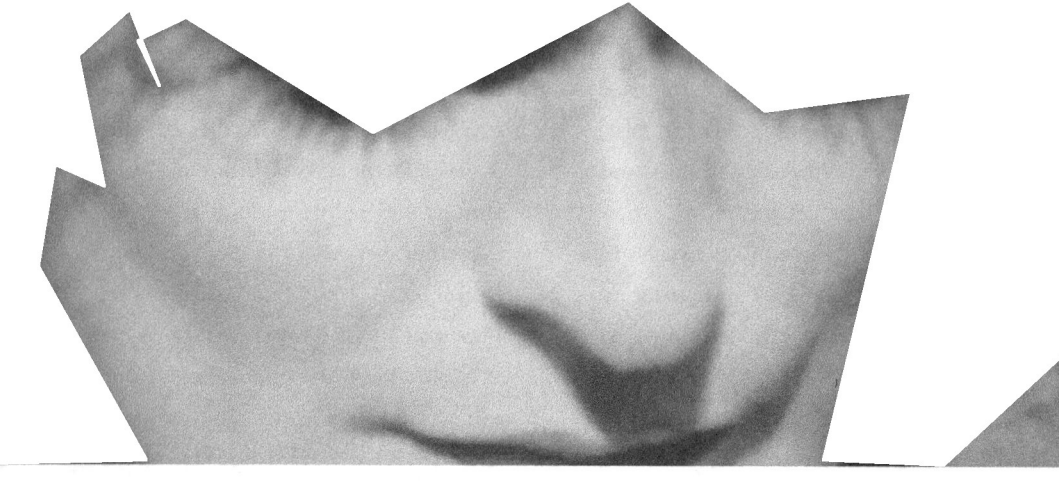

BERNICE STEGERS

RECALLS THE MAKING OF THE UNDERRATED MASTERPIECE

Bernice Stegers was only 28 when Fellini cast her in CITY OF WOMEN. In a chat we had for a 2020 documentary on Marcello Mastroianni, here are highlights of that revealing interview, covering Fellini, the wonder of Cinecitta, working alongside the legendary Marcello Mastroianni and life on set with a true filmmaking icon.

How did you get the part of the woman on the train?

Well Fellini had offered me another part in Casanova, but I couldn't do it because I was doing a TV series for Thames. Then he asked to see me again but I couldn't, because I was unusually on a yacht in the Caribbean. But later I went to see him, spent the day with him and he offered me the part. You know, it was all exciting being in Cinecitta. What I recall about my first day of shooting, was being told by Fellini and everyone there that I was incredibly beautiful, perfect in fact, and then I arrived in make up at 6 and it was not until 9, three hours later, that they had eradicated all the flaws they saw in me. It was quite amazing. That happened every morning, three hours in make up, with every bit of hair being curled. What I remember most about first meeting Marcello was his beef about having to be on a diet. Federico said if you are playing an intellectual you have to be slim. He also had to have all his body hair waxed off, so I remember him spending a lot of the morning being all itchy.

Was your first day filming on the train then?

Yes I think it was the train. That was all effect, you know. It was a false train being bumped up and down by these big guys. There was miles of painted landscapes being rolled across the windows. There was a lot of incense, church incense. Whenever I smell it now, wow! So the men were bumping the carriage on the big logs.

You can not imagine. Being on that train was more like being on a real train, like some dream.

Would it not have been easier to just film on a real train do you think? I suppose he did want that artificial look though didn't he?

I know. I am not sure actually though. The whole thing was about having control of every bit of it. When we did go out to film the first bits, the palaver of that with the lights and watering the trees in the boiling hot weather.... I think that was more of a fuss than if it was in a studio. Plus Cinecitta was Fellini's world, they were all at his disposal.

What was it like acting with Mastroianni on the first day? Was it a natural experience?

Oh no, I mean I had to kiss him on the train. I did have this moment where I thought I am going to kiss this man who is the heart throb of Europe. I had to really pull myself together. Marcello had to bang on the door in the bathroom scene and say "Were your husbands not very virile?" But what he said was "Your husbands weren't wery wirile?" And I just could not... (Laughs)... I could not... I must have corpsed about four times whenever he came to this line. That took the edge off kissing him.

But he was such an icon though wasn't he? This was about twenty years since La Dolce Vita.

Yes, late seventies or so. He was still very beautiful, and he kept his career going. He was a very good actor, a marvellous being. He was kind of "action" and he was free, freer than off stage in fact. I also spent time with him off stage too, going on about this coffee and cigarette diet, going on about his favourite Italian soup. He would sort of dribble thinking about it.

To me he looks just like he did in 8 1/2 in City of Women...

Yeah. Marvellous looking man, nicely lit.

Acting with him, once you got over the kissing thing, was it natural?

Absolutely. He was an actor's actor. He didn't go in for the method, talking about acting or it being difficult, anything what he called rubbish. But actually, it was about that freedom. He let himself into it.

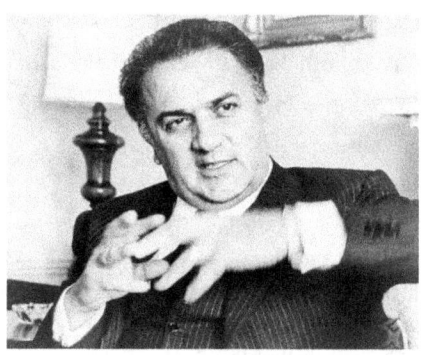

He always said making a film was like a playground with Fellini...

Oh yeah, the two of them, yeah. They had endless jokes about their cocks. Every morning was a whole malarkey, gags and jokes. Well Marcello was entirely in Fellini's hands. His mother would come and have lunch with us and she would berate Fellini about not working with Marcello more often, saying he'd made him the man he was and it had taken twenty years to work with him again. But they slipped in together like they were wearing an old jumper. Marcello would have done anything for him. Well he did do anything he wanted him to!

It must be amazing to look back on working with fellas like Fellini and Mastroianni. I know you have worked with so many people...

Well no one like them! Fellini used to take me out on a night to the circus after the show. He was keen on the lion tamer, all those things that sound clichéd now. I was 28, going to the big top with Fellini, sitting and eating with the performers. It was amazing. And then the people who would turn up, like Sartre, anyone passing through Rome would come and have lunch. And Fellini would have a guy come from Rimini with the new season's snails, the Rimini dish. I mean, the leisure, the schedule. The film took months. Massive sets were built. I had just fallen in love with a director and was very aware of schedule and budget, but Fellini's world had none of this. Eight months it took to shoot. I don't think anyone knew how to say no. I wonder if films like Casanova made any money. I know Amarcord made money, but I am not so sure about the others. He must have been bailed out by benefactors and the studios.

What are your memories of the big feminist scene? That is such a massive sequence.

God, I had three blouses made because it was the summer and I got so hot in my suit that the white blouse got dark with sweat. I think I had the fur hat on as well. I must have been about 100 degrees. I think I did like 30 or 40 takes. Someone would come on and whip the blouse off and change it. I remember people

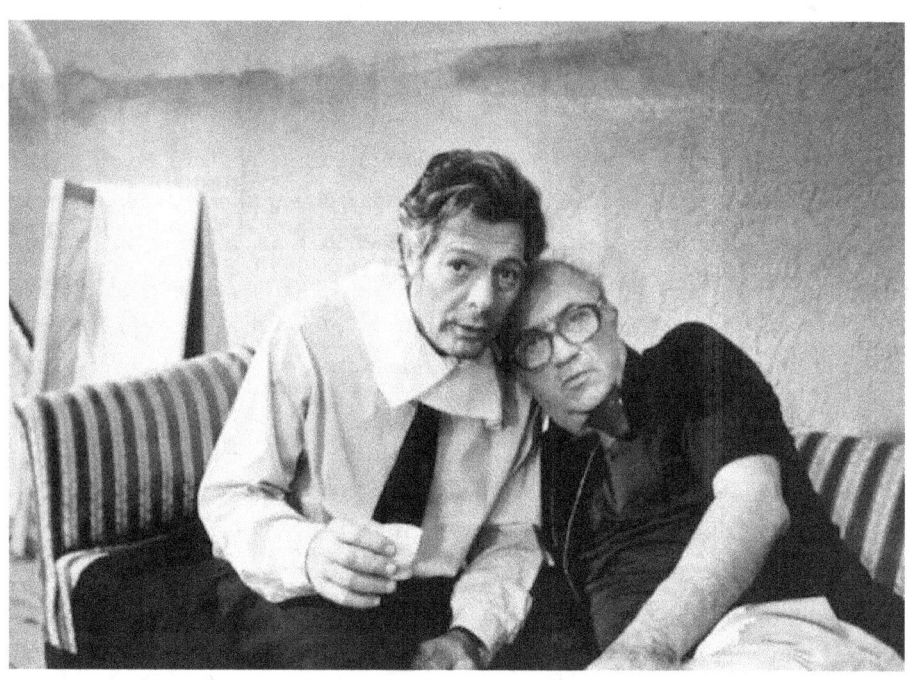

saying keep doing it, keep doing it. I think it took days.

And Fellini always had his megaphone there too?

Yeah. He was very charming over the megaphone. And because we didn't do synch sound, he had wonderful music playing. The script was neither here nor there for him. When I asked him for the script for my speech, he thought that was a piece of acting nonsense. He just wanted me to speak passionately. It was all dubbed afterwards as well. Italians didn't care if the mouth as in synch, it was all about watching the eyes to them.

So do you think City of Women is quite a confused film?

Yes I do actually; I think it's a right mess. I never found out what happened really. I was supposed to be a thread that ran all the way through it. But at a certain point, Fellini fell for a very gorgeous extra who had an exquisite body and he became obsessed with her. She gave an interview about them having an affair and all this kind of stuff. So this all made a kind of mess. I was sent home and recalled to do the last scene on the train. I never found out what happened.

It would have made a lot more sense had your character run through the whole thing.

Yes it would have. I was employed for 8 months and not used. But I could not get a straight answer. Fellini was making it up as he went along, having all these sets built. So somewhere in the middle of all this, with this girl and me being sent home...

Do you think he tried to fit too much in there?

Yes. I mean the film was a failure. Critics gave it a kind of "Thanks but no thanks". I haven't seen it for years. Such a shame actually. But I was thinking, I was 28 when we made it and Fellini was like 60. I took me twenty years or something to realise he fancied me something rotten. But that would literally have never occurred to me. It was like my dad or something. I mean, however old you are, add another thirty years, you wouldn't expect someone that much older to be thinking that. It would be so far out of your mind! I was fancying men of thirty then. I mean, the thought of Fellini... It never crossed my mind; which was quite good really, because it never got dodgy and awkward for me.

Maybe he liked that you were not going to be easy for him.

Very, very possibly, yes. And it's fairly well known now that Fellini had an affair with Germaine Greer and my character was based on her. So that was interesting as well.

END.

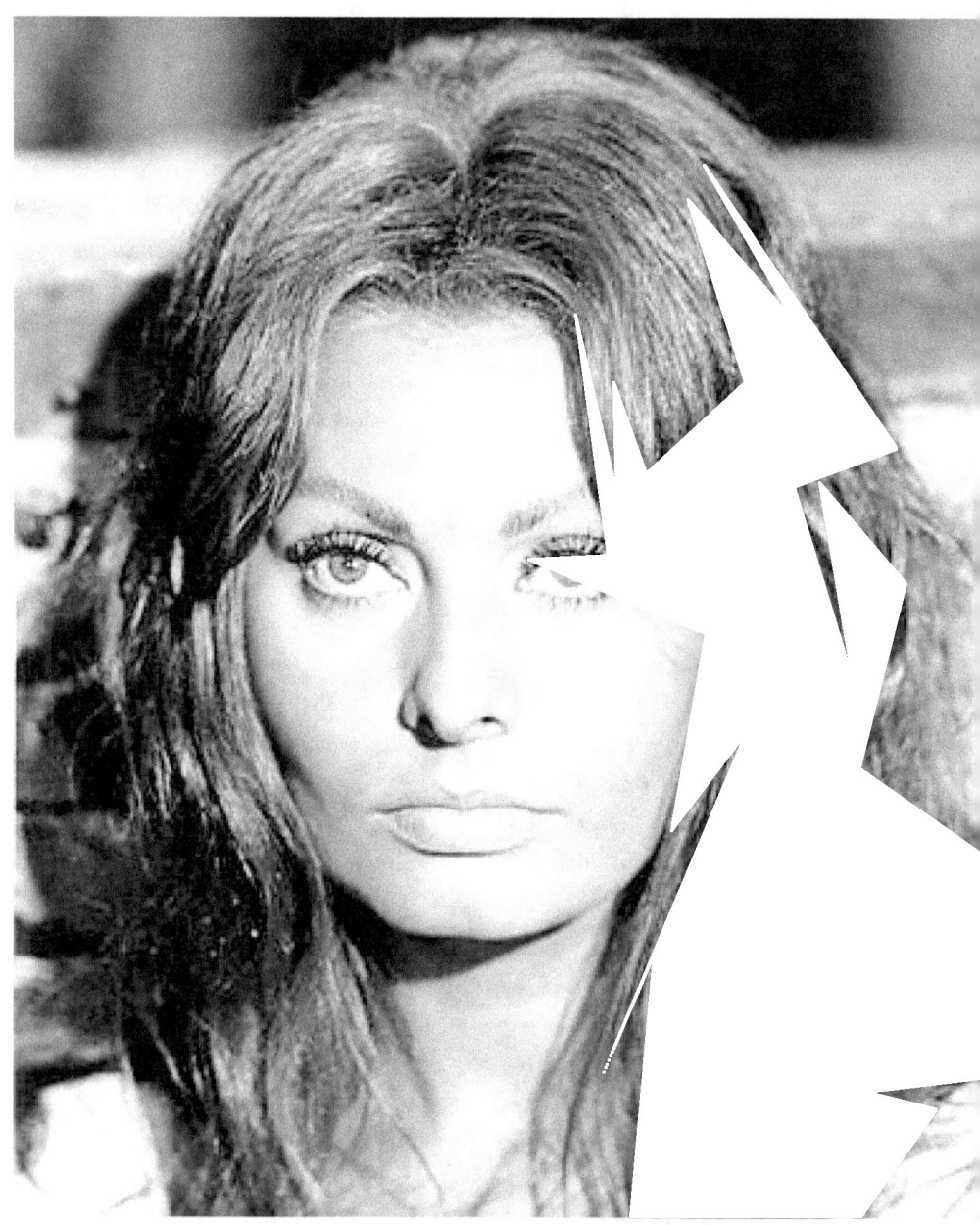

SOPHIA LOREN
The Golden Years
CELEBRATING THE CLASSIC ERA OF THE ITALIAN ICON'S REMARKABLE CAREER

Sophia Loren represents a long gone era, a time when a Hollywood star could be both hugely glamorous and totally relatable on a human level, when their humour and honesty shone through while their stardom remained undimmed. This was an age when stars were stars, and though it's a tired cliché to state such a thing, Loren represents the highest calibre of such a celebrity. She was famous not for being famous; she was put on her pedestal for being both one of the world's most beautiful women and among its finest actresses. You got the impression, and still do, that her humanity was always a major part of her uniqueness. She was paradoxically both an out of reach beauty and a firmly rooted Italian who never forgot her working class roots.

We've all heard the "rags to riches" tale, the story of a transcendent fame that came from humble beginnings, and it's often a biographical element exaggerated for publicity's sake, or to make the star in question appear more down to earth to their legions of fans. But Sophia Loren really did have such a tale, and this was no minor detail to provide back story to her film career. Her journey is a well documented rise to fame, though the word "rags" seems to belittle the beginnings in Italy of which Sophia has always been so very proud. Her humble childhood, at times extremely tough, not only made her iconic fame so spectacular, it also ensured her audience understood her all the more, both idolised and related to her. It's a balance that seems contradictory but in fact makes perfect sense.

The fact that Sophia Loren is still around, still there making the odd appearance on screen and in public, is extraordinary. Her name alone and the very idea of her belongs to a golden period, yet her finest performances and greatest cinematic achievements have not aged, seem to have lived on long after the classic era has ended, and remain as vital and impactful as ever before. Whether she was providing the glamour in a Hollywood hit or representing the earthy, ethereal qualities of the women of her homeland, Italy, Loren convinced and dazzled no matter what. In these films she seems to transcend the flat screen she inhabits and sets foot into the real world. You could say the same about many of the golden age's legendary stars, but with Loren it seems truer somehow. Perhaps it's because she was always so down to earth, so self depreciating without

false modesty, despite her extraordinary fame and success.

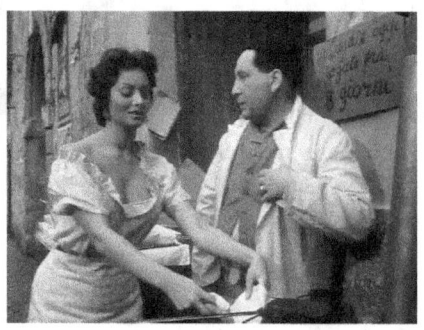

She had been making films in Italy for a number of years when she suddenly emerged, as the Superstar Loren, in Vittorio De Sica's The Gold of Naples in 1954. The Gold of Naples is very much De Sica's homage to Naples, the place he grew up in, and to show his adoration for that special city he explores its multi faceted beauty (as he would with Rome in Yesterday, Today and Tomorrow) in a series of cinematic stories, all portraying the vitality and energy of Naples. Again, it was an anthology film, something the Italian cinema masters did so well, and each tale is as entertaining and provocative as the last. One centres on the interactions between a criminal and a clown, while Loren's instalment (entitled Pizza a cedito), in my view the most successful, involves her playing a character named Sofia funnily enough, in a quest for her lost wedding ring. Loren is excellent as the fiery and charismatic young woman, a fireball of energy and passion, and having several scenes which were destined to go down in her legend. Perhaps the most memorable of all is the famous "walking the street in the rain" scene, definitely the first iconic sequence of her career, cementing her movements into the everlasting canon of European and world cinema.

De Sica and Loren had acted together in a previous film, so Gold of Naples was a consolidation of their union. She said of their pairing on The Gold of Naples: "Perhaps De Sica was really impressed by me, because when he saw me and realized that I am a Neapolitan, he started talking Neapolitan with me and we had a nice conversation. He was looking for a young woman to play the role of the pizza maker in the movie and

that became my first role (for him)…"

De Sica and Loren would make more and even greater films together, though this was a brilliant start to their working relationship and immortal off screen friendship.

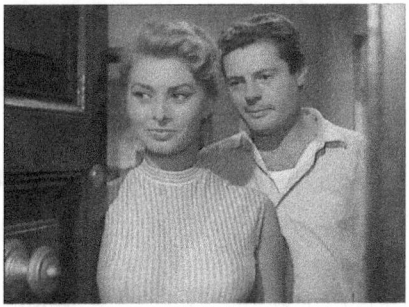

In 1955, Sophia Loren made one of her most important early films, Too Bad She's Bad, which was directed by Alessandro Blasetti. Billed with her name before the title, it was clear by now that Loren was becoming, quite quickly it must be said, a star in her own country. She was already a drawer at the box office and it's said male cinema goers flocked to her pictures to catch Loren in all her glory.

Here, Loren plays Lina, a con woman who teams up with two other criminals to rip off tax driver Paolo out of both his cab and all the money he's earned. One of the things which makes this relatively small film extra special is that Paolo the cabbie is played by the great Marcello Mastroianni. Sophia and Marcello would go on to make some of the most memorable Italian films in history together, but Too Bad She's Bad is the beginning of their wonderful collaboration. From the word go it seems there was a special chemistry between the pair, and their scenes together here are slightly better than the film they are actually acting in, though the film itself is wonderful too. It's understandable that their friendship would extend into real life and in her autobiography she has very kind words about the great man. On screen however, there is a unique simpatico, almost as if they were made for each other. Marcello's charisma shines off the screen, while Loren seems to be even more fiery and radiant whenever paired with him. He is down to earth and honest,

she spunky and mistrustful. Both are wonderfully playful in their roles.

Too Bad She's Bad moves along nicely, is neatly directed and the script is straight forward and funny in a simple way. It is, however, the acting which elevates it, especially from Marcello and Loren, the latter looking, it has to be said, extremely striking. The film may be overlooked these days, but it's vitally important in her on screen development.

Sophia was extraordinarily busy in the mid fifties, appearing in film after film in her native Italy. Produced by Ponti, De Laurentiis and Basilio Franchina, The River Girl was the latest visual treat to feature the ever growingly popular Loren. She plays Nives, a peasant girl who finds out she is expecting a child just as her lover abandons her. But it turns out the guy crossed the wrong girl and to act out her vengeance she reports him to the authorities for being a smuggler. Later, the police officer Enzo, who carries a torch for Nives, finds her working as a cutter to support her one parent family.

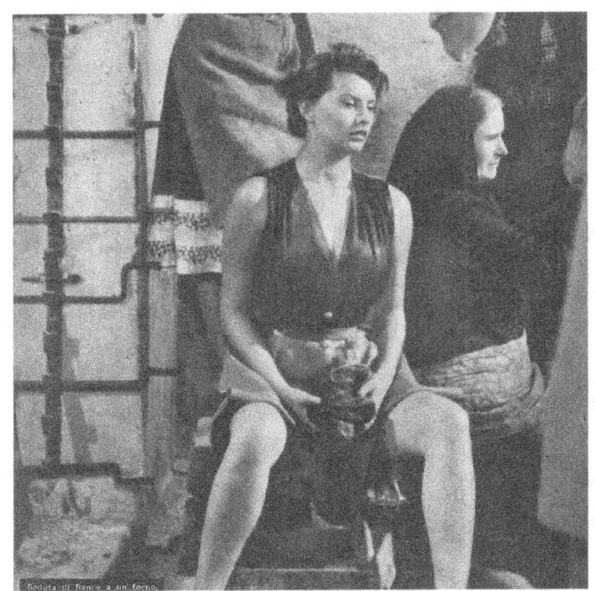

Caduta di fronte a un forno

descent in the opening reels. In many ways it lures one into a false sense of security and then delivers the blow. It begins lightly enough and one would suspect a lively Italian love farce is on its way. But with its increasingly dark themes and heavy tone it is in extreme harsh contrast to the more light hearted fare Loren had been taking part in around the same time.

Concerned that her ex lover has escaped from prison, he offers to protect her but she declines. The film ends in a tragedy that jars somewhat with the rest of the film, but delivers an impactful punch that puts a poignant and darkly ironic end to the tale.

The River Girl, also known as Woman of the River, is something of a dark horse, a deceiving Italian obscurity. It has a rustic, frill-free appearance about it, but it does not suggest even a hint of its dark

Still, Loren is presented to us as exotic beauty, a temptress paradoxically tempted by her dangerous lover and then having to pay the price for letting her guard down. She carries the film with an apparent ease, her charisma hiding the cracks in the slow moving plot and the often creaky dialogue. Gerard Oury is rather stiff but competent as the policeman, and Rik Battaglia is suitably mistrustful as Gino, the outlaw lover. Still, it's Loren's show and she is highly watchable and likeable as the woman in this messy predicament. Modern viewers used to spandex clad superheroes fighting with robots might find The River Girl slow and inconsequential, but it's an engaging film despite its aged quality, and often because of its antiquated charm. It's also worth watching because it presents one of the first times Loren carries a feature on her back, looking beautiful and one hundred percent the "peasant girl" Italian style, and demonstrates fully that she was a star in the making. In many ways a precursor to the kind of heavy drama she proved she could pull off in Two Women, five years later. A real hidden gem, this one.

It wasn't long before Hollywood and the movie moguls across the sea noticed the appeal of the rising Italian superstar, seeing great potential in the earthy, charismatic beauty and fighting for her presence in their glossy productions. Loren took to Hollywood naturally, supplying their films with the required glamour and sassiness, though one could argue that she

never really matched the roles she took in Italy, the more raw and gritty ones, in the more shallow landscape of American film.

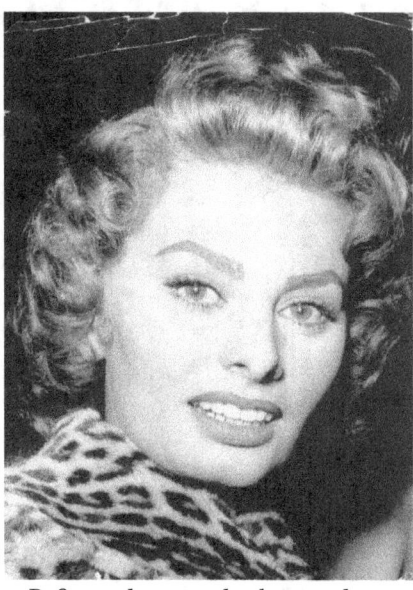

Before the much better known Pride and the Passion (released the same year) cemented her fame in Hollywood, Sophia had already appeared in a film which became a major contribution to her iconic status as a legendary beauty. In Boy on a Dolphin, the first movie she made speaking English, she makes a highly memorable first appearance. Popping up out of the sea and climbing on to a rickety old sail boat, in terms of movie entrances she rivals Ursula Andress in Dr No emerging from the sea, though in my opinion it's a much more magical unveiling. Though she was already known in Italy and had given the world many fine moments in movies over there already (think of her walk alone in Too Bad She's Bad and her riveting performance in The River Girl), Boy on a Dolphin today looks like the true arrival of a legend, when the world was awakened to the charms of the Italian goddess.

Boy on a Dolphin is far from being one of the finest films Sophia made in her classic era, but it's a fun and exotic romantic adventure, establishing her as a star to take notice of. Co starring Alan Ladd, and based on David Divine's novel, it tells the tale of a Greek diver (Loren) on the island of Hydra, who finds an ancient statue and gets entangled with potential buyers when attempting to sell the relic. The plot is rather silly but the adventure pulls you in and it is aided by the film's technical sharpness. The music by Hugo Friedhofer adds some authentic atmosphere (he received an Oscar nomination for his score), while director Jean Negulesco uses the opportunity to not only photograph the elements and awe-inspiring scenery, but Loren herself, who he presents to us as some great Greek figure, a Goddess if you like.

Though Carlo Ponti led the way for her and ensured she got the best deals in the best possible films, Loren has been insistent that fame comes from talent, and is the destiny of all those born to be a star. "You do not become a star, you are born a star," she told Alain Elkann, adding, "A star is born with that indefinable extra something. Actually, truth be told, I do not know if I really am a big star. And in fact that is not the most important thing for me. What counts in life is to bring about more of your own dreams. In such a way that your life becomes like a fairy tale. This is what has happened to me, it is just like that."

There is truth in her words. Think of Loren's earliest roles in Italy, barely into her twenties, and one can already see that she radiates. Yes, she sharpened her skills as the years went on, but that raw talent was there all along, that otherness which blesses all unique people.

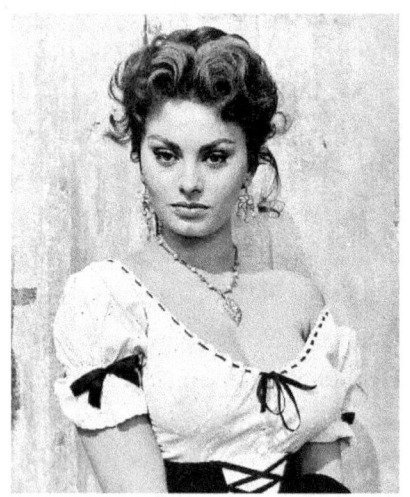

The earthiness is evident in her earliest Hollywood films, that wonderful, open naivety she harbours when interacting with fellow Italians. Here though, in the lavish world of movie stars and big budgets, she was out of her comfort zone. Still, she entered this world with ease. One of the first films to truly make her a household name was 1957's The Pride and the Passion, which cast her alongside two men who were already legendary at the time, Frank Sinatra and Cary Grant. Grant and Sinatra are good enough in their roles, sparking off genuinely believable rivalry, but the film belongs to Loren, fresh faced and vital, not to mention young enough to be both men's daughter, who snatches it from under their feet, though given Loren is a generous and sharing kind of performer, showboating was perhaps not on her mind. Yet her straight forward charisma and physicality alone were enough to ensure a film stealing performance. That said, it's in the control, the technicalities, the intelligence and intuitiveness where Loren truly excels. She does as the script says, provides the love interest, but her qualities are too bewitching for her to be a mere distraction from the plot. Many people will remember The Pride and the Passion for Sophia alone, and in particular the highly memorable dance scene which has become one of the most legendary sequences in Loren's filmography. It's a truly sexy moment in film history, but the sexiness is subtle, more down to suggestion than crudity. Loren has complete control of herself, clearly feels the music cursing through her veins, and channels it through her body. No wonder all the onlookers are stunned, with Grant in particular reduced to a gawping zombie.

The year of 1957 was a memorable one for Sophia Loren, and the same year she co starred with stars like Alan Ladd, Frank Sinatra and Cary Grant, she found herself sharing the screen the screen with that most American of institutions, John Wayne himself. Though you would be hard pressed to find two actors who - apparently at least - fit together less than Wayne, the macho Western hero and Loren, the rootsy Italian goddess, weirdly they do not seem alien to one another in Legend of the Lost, a lavish, handsomely shot, big budgetted production.

In some respects, the following year was even stronger for Loren. Spending more time in Hollywood,

she cemented her position as one of the world's leading actresses, and it was at this point that the American studios began to let her display her formidable acting talents, as well as her Mediterranean beauty.

Desire Under the Elms paired her with Anthony Perkins. Based on Eugene O'Neill's play, the story takes place on a farm ruled by the ruthless Ephraim Cabot, who leaves two dead wives behind him and is on to his third, a beautiful young Italian named Anna, played by Loren. Anthony Perkins is Eben, the son hoping to take the farm off the old tyrant who says he would rather see it burn than leave it to anyone. Eben and Anna begin an affair, which is serious enough until Anna falls pregnant to him, though the ageing farmer believes the child is his. The stress and pressure between the three parties mounts and results in the darkest of tragedy, with Anna jumping to a nightmarish conclusion to keep the love of the younger man.

Desire Under the Elms is perhaps the finest American film Loren appeared in at this time. Weighty, heavily dramatic and not afraid to go to truly dark places, it gave Loren another opportunity to show her audience she was not just some curvy vixen to be gawped at, but a serious actress capable of truly brilliant things. The whole cast dazzle in Desire Under the Elms, but Sophia seems to be on a whole different level, being both hopelessly naive and conniving at the same time. It's a balancing act she pulls off brilliantly. It's also a credit to her that even so early into her Hollywood career she wasn't afraid of going for something un-commercial and a character that was hardly a saint. It's clear she's trying hard here, perhaps in a bid to prove she was a force to be reckoned with.

A more forgotten film was The Black Orchid, which paired her for the second time with Anthony Quinn. Again, Loren is wonderful in the film as Rose Bianco, the widow of a gangster who meets Frank (Quinn), a man struggling with life after losing his wife. So quickly into her career overseas, Loren was winning rave notices and, in the case of The Black Orchid, serious attention from award committees when the Venice Film Festival gave her the Best Actress award for her understated efforts. Though the film rarely gets singled out as a highlight from late 50s American cinema, it has stood the test of time well and Loren's work in it is among her finest feats of the period. She also works brilliantly with Quinn, who is at his most sensitive.

And then there was Houseboat, in which she co starred once again with Cary Grant. Given that their brief association had ended when The Pride and the Passion wrapped up, there were, quite naturally, minor problems on the set of Houseboat. Grant was desperate to reignite their relationship, but Loren was firmly tied to Ponti by then, adamant, much to Grant's annoyance, that she had made the right choice.

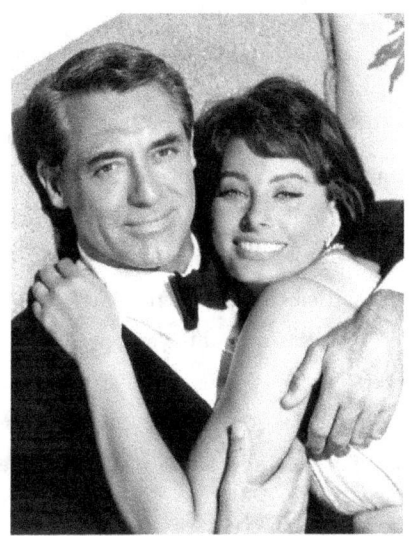

The film itself is one of the more light and fluffy films Loren made in her golden Hollywood era, the tale of a widower (Grant) who with his three children sets up home on a run down houseboat with their nanny, a charismatic Sophia Loren. The main reason to watch Houseboat is for the undeniable chemistry between Grant and Loren; indeed, one would have to be blind to miss the sparks that fly between them on screen, and given the bitterness between their parting on the previous film it's a wonder Grant could pull himself together. But pull himself together he

certainly does, and he matches Loren's exotic qualities with his relatable warmth.

Compared to her roles in films like The Black Orchid, Desire Under the Elms and the later Two Women, Houseboat is like a walk in the park. She is undeniably appealing however and it must have been a nice breath of fresh air for Loren herself, who had been in some pretty downbeat pictures in the run up to this glossy, slightly corny but hugely enjoyable Hollywood romance. Loren also has one of her most famous screen moments in Houseboat, when she sings the classic Bing Bang Bong number.

One of Loren's more iconic and suitably fitting roles came opposite Clark Gable in the wonderful It Started in Naples, a romantic comedy in which Sophia expressed her more playful side, which was refreshing after some more gloomy Hollywood pictures. She was full once again of the kind of spirit so often illustrated in her films with Vittorio De Sica, who funnily enough appears in the cast as an actor. Sophia plays a sexy nightclub dancer who is taking care of her nephew, whose father has just died. The deceased man's brother is an American lawyer (played by Clark Gable) who travels to Naples, objects to the boy's situation and wishes to bring him home to the States. Of course, with the female being the bewitching Sophia Loren, it's not long before a fondness forms, and she and the lawyer end up slipping into a romance.

Gable was at the very end of his career and life here, and It Started in Naples was both his first colour film and last to be released while he was still alive. Needless to say he went out on a high, and though considerably older than Loren, he works convincingly, and quite wonderfully, opposite her. The laid back American and the fiery Italian make a great duo, and their sparring is both believable and hugely entertaining. For me, this is one of Loren's finest early performances in America; she is charisma personified and dazzles on the screen. The song and dance scenes in the club are spectacular, and though her act lacks the subtle grace of, say, a Dietrich number, her wild antics and stunning appearance make her certainly more eye catching. In short, she puts in a superb performance in both the dramatic/comedic scenes and when on stage as a flamboyant performer. She received a Golden Globe nomination for her part, though in all fairness she should surely have won the gong.

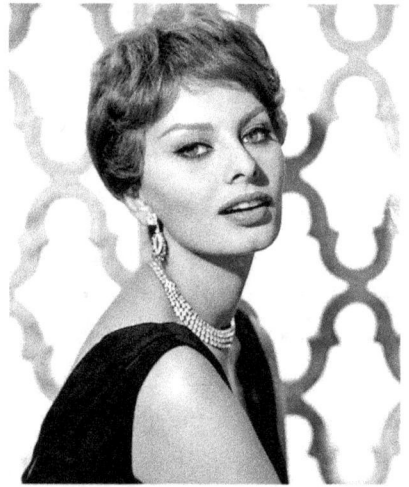

The same year she put Clark Gable under her spell, Loren did the same to another icon in The Millionairess, opposite Peter Sellers. Based on

George Bernard Shaw's 1936 play, the film is genuinely funny, with both Loren and Sellers at the top of their games. Loren, though usually best suited to more earthy types, excels as the spoilt heiress who cannot marry her suitor unless he can transform

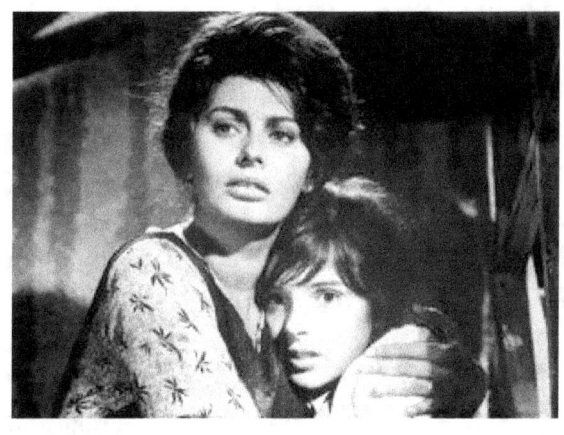

500 pounds into 15,000. When the relationship falls through, Loren tries to kill herself by jumping in the Thames River. Sellers is Dr. Amhed el Kabir, a kind hearted Indian doctor who enters the plot, and though his accent and performance in general might be called un-PC today, it is an affectionate portrayal of an Indian.

The end of 1960 saw the release of a film which may represent the very zenith of Loren's career as a dramatic actress, Two Women, a harrowing and compelling drama directed by the great Vittorio De Sica. Based on the novel by Alberto Moravia, the story draws from what the Italians call the Marocchinate, the horrific events in Rome during the Second World War when innocents were killed and raped in their masses. Importantly, as Hollywood often has with its cynical money spinning ways, Two Women does not set out to make entertainment from the horror, but depict it with truth and a certain brutality it no doubt calls for.

Loren plays Cesira, a widowed shopkeeper, who with her young daughter Rosetta (Eleanora Brown) flees to central Italy to escape the Rome bombings. There they meet Michele (Jean-Paul Belmondo), an educated radical communist with his own ideas about sociological changes, who develops a strong relationship with both mother and daughter.

While holed up with other refugees, Michele develops a love for Cesira, though she claims to be too busy looking out for her daughter to care about any possible romances. One day when a group of German soldiers arrive, demanding what little food the Italian peasants have for themselves, they force Michele to guide them through the traitorous Italian hills, and despite the general panic of the gathered refugees, he promises to return that evening. Young Rosetta is particularly distraught, as she had begun to view him as a kind of father.

 Soon the bombings spread to the hills and Cesira realises she and her daughter must return to Rome, where things are beginning to ease off a little. When the pair learn that Rome has been recaptured by the Allied troops, they travel cross country to head back but are targeted by Moroccan soldiers who gang rape and brutalise them in a truly harrowing but devastatingly powerful sequence. The child has her innocence snatched from her by this most brutal and careless of acts, while the bond between mother and daughter suffers serious damage. Yet despite this merciless horror, and the destruction of her childhood, their bond proves unbreakable. In the end, when Rosetta learns of Michele's murder by the Germans, she is embraced by her mother in a pure and beautiful fashion, proving their love is immortal and cannot be torn apart by the devastations of war and the downfall of humanity itself.

Two Women is a superb film, that kind of rare cinematic experience where everything - literally everything - is perfectly aligned and delivered with integrity; from the direction and the cinematography, to the script and the acting, every inch of this film is done with a passion, often overwhelmingly so, and extremely effective. It is however, when all is said and done, Loren herself who impresses the most. When Carlo Ponti bought the film rights in the late 1950s, he was destined for Loren to be in the movie, though not initially as the mother.

The elder role was set to go to Anna Magnani, while Sophia was going to portray the girl. Original director George Cukor was intending to take the film on as part of his deal with Paramount, but when they both dropped out of the project, Ponti hired De Sica instead, who had already worked wonders with Sophia in earlier movies. When Magnani opted out, Loren took the mother role, aging herself a decade in the process, and the much younger Eleonora Brown was signed up as the daughter, in De Sica's view, for "better opportunity to stress, to underline, the monstrous impact of war on people. The historical truth is that the great majority of those raped were young girls." It may have been a shocking decision for the time, but it made the film much more authentic, much more courageous, and infinitely more powerful.

Eleonora recently claimed in an interview that it was Loren who protected her from the harshness of the rape scene, and that in order to achieve the required emotion for the finale (when the girl learns of some devastating news), De Sica told Eleonora that her parents had just died. The method may have worked, judging by her hysteria in the closing reels, but it would result in a court case in this day and age.

Loren herself, experienced by now, did not need directorial tricks to ensure she reached the dizzying emotional heights required of her for the role. Speaking later, she said she was inspired by her mother's own bravery during the horrific war. In an interview in the 1970s, Loren commented, "The book was one of the most beautiful I've ever read. I thought it was worth taking the risk at 25 to play an older woman because the story was so beautiful."

It is a staggering performance, rich and bold, daring and brave, easily among the finest film performances of that or any other era. Deservedly, she won the Best Actress Oscar for her efforts, vitally being the first foreign actress to do so. She also won a BAFTA, a Cannes Film Festival

Best Actress Award, and numerous other honours.

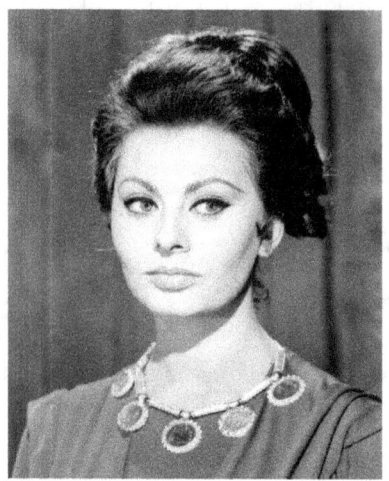

Of the news she was nominated for the Oscar, Loren recalled, "I didn't expect to be nominated, because generally the Academy doesn't nominate anything that wasn't done in the English language. Reading the papers, I saw that people were saying, 'Maybe Sophia Loren is going to win.' I said, 'Listen, if I don't win, of course I'm going to be a little bit upset, but I'm happy to be among the five nominees.' I thought, 'If I win, I think I'm going to faint, and I think I better faint at home than onstage' — so I didn't go. I really didn't think I was going to win. I was in Italy at home. Of course, with the change of time in Italy and America, we made a mistake and at 6 a.m. said, 'Well, the ceremony is over' and went to bed. The next thing you know, Cary Grant is calling and saying, 'Sophia — you won, you won!' After I found out, I smoked a cigarette."

Recently, Loren commented that Two Women seems to be a firm favourite of fans. "They always ask me about Two Women. Often people feel very close and intimate with the films I've made — but especially the relationship between the mother and daughter in Two Women. They're really in it with you. I think it's a beautiful thing, that people can feel they know you through the films you make."

For Loren it was a case of surpassing her sex symbol beginnings and becoming a serious actor. Speaking to Dougie Thompson much later, she said of her initial sex appeal, "I liked it because I was doing it in a joking kind of way. And I knew that it was a preparation for what I would do later on. It's impossible to be a sex symbol all your life. You have to be terribly young and then your career is very short. so at some point you have to choose roles that you can go further with. That's what I did when I made Two Women -- I was 25 and I played the mother of a 15-year-old girl. I really established myself as an actress with that and then I had wonderful roles."

When I think of Two Women, key scenes come racing through my mind; Loren and Brown snuggling in bed together; the horrifying rape scene; Loren in the middle of the road, broken, bare kneed on the gravel. That said, it is the whole film which must be remembered. Two Women is certainly a raw film, but there really was no other way to play it without being untrue to Italy's war time legacy and the horror experienced by so many innocent people. Loren's gut wrenchingly gritty performance is so heartfelt one imagines she has been through this herself, and the fact she was channelling her own mother's struggles, and her childhood memories, explains why the portrayal is so painfully believable. It could be argued that few actors, male or female, achieved such raw, naked anguish on the screen ever again.

Remarkably, given her huge fame at the time, Loren was able to juggle roles in her native Italy, taking on lower budget fare, with bigger, glitzy Hollywood productions. The year after she stunned the movie going world with Two Women - itself much more than a mere movie - she provided the glamour and beauty in the epic El Cid opposite film icon Charlton Heston, which unlike Two Women was entertainment pure and simple.

Loren was put to much better use in Christian Jacque's Madame (1961), a co production between Spain, Italy and France. Playing a typically bold laundress, Loren is at her purest and most earthy, excelling as the uneducated, down to earth woman who falls for a sergeant who becomes the Marshal of France. It's a vital, energetic performance, in complete contrast to her glorified, subtle, nuanced yet strangely underwhelming effort in the same year's El Cid.

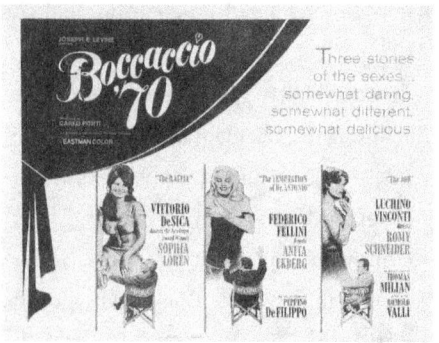

In 1962, Loren was reunited with Vittorio De Sica once again for their own instalment in the anthology film Boccaccio 70, a lively and hilarious comedy in the style of writer and poet Giovanni Boccaccio, which also featured stories by Luchino Visconti, Federico Fellini and Mario Monicelli.

Boccaccio 70 is playful and wonderfully over the top, with each Italian master relishing the opportunity to throw away subtlety and inhibitions all together. De Sica's instalment is full of life, and so infectiously good natured that the mob of sex hungry men marching towards Sophia like starving hounds, who would be threatening in other surroundings, come across as loveable rogues rather than the sexist relics they really are. In the face of their collective desperation however Sophia is empowered, a beautiful, statuesque woman who knows that even a glimpse of her leg will send them into a wild frenzy. But she cannot be owned or had for any amount of money. It has to be said that, though Loren is often beautiful in her films, she is extremely sexy in Boccaccio 70. But looks aside, the real skill is in the spot-on portrayal of this quintessential spirited Italian, unwilling to be gawped at and auctioned off like a mere play thing.

Whenever Loren teamed up with De Sica, the results were always special. However, when she happened to get together with both De Sica and the wonderful Marcello Mastroianni, the films became magical. Perhaps their finest work as a threesome was Yesterday, Today and Tomorrow, another iconic Loren film (perhaps her most iconic of all) in which she displayed both her timeless beauty and her versatility as an actress.

The film consists of three separate stories, each one presenting a different aspect of Loren's multi faceted public persona. In the first story she is the down to earth Italian mother, selling cigarettes on the black market to support her husband, the great Mastroianni. Fined by the authorities, the whole village get together by hiding her furniture so it will not be repossessed. When the threat of prison looms, Loren falls pregnant, for by Italian law no woman expecting a child

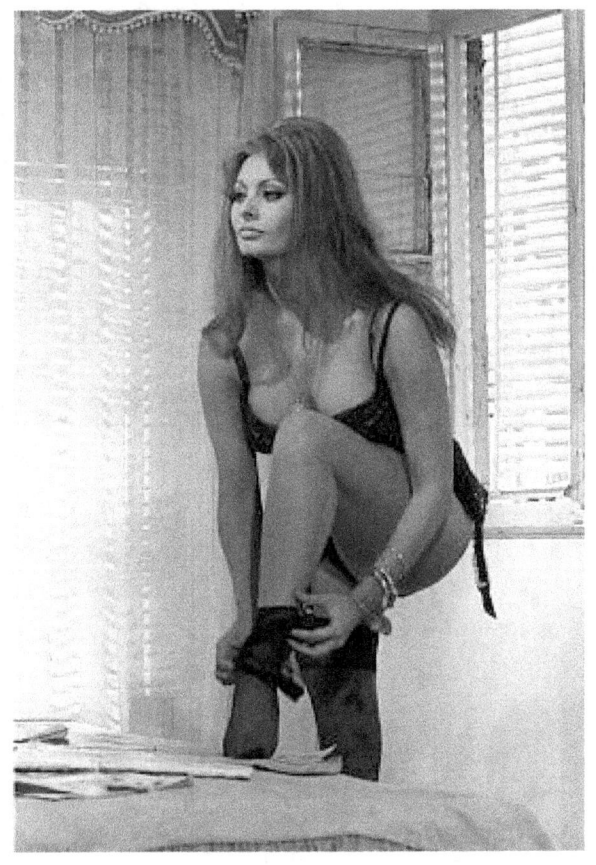

can be locked up. She repeats the ploy for seven years running, having child after child and exhausting her husband to the point of near mental collapse. When he refuses to impregnate her again out of sheer exhaustion, she accepts her fate and is imprisoned. Showing their loyalty once again, her friends and neighbours gather together as much money as possible to pay her bail and attempt to get her a pardon, after the success of which she is freed and reunited with her family.

This instalment is very much a celebration of Italy and its decent,

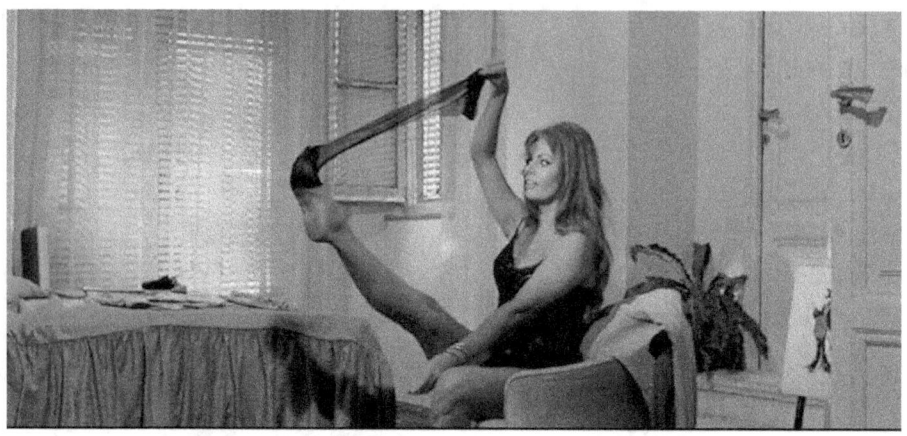

honest, loyal people. Working together, they look out for one another, very much against the system and willing to do whatever it takes for the man or woman next door. Loren embodies this now rare breed of woman wonderfully, being both hilarious and formidable as the gutsy Adelina, tired and put upon by her difficult life but too stubborn to give into the law, until that is the situation becomes impossible. Marcello is excellent too, and the pair work off of each other splendidly.

The second story features Loren as Anna, the wife of a rich industrialist who takes a ride with her lover Renzo (Mastroianni) and must choose between her fondness for Renzo and the material riches her husband can provide. Renzo hates the greedy side of her, and though drawn to her beauty is put off by her materialistic shallowness. Following an incident which damages her precious Rolls Royce, Renzo sees her for what she is and his mind is made up for him. Loren excels yet again in a part that could not be more different to the woman she plays in the first story. Empty, callous and vein, Loren makes the woman so believable it's hard to accept she is the same actress who only a matter of minutes earlier was bringing the pure Adelina to life before our eyes.

The third part of the film has become the most famous, in which she plays Mora, a prostitute who works from her Rome apartment and finds herself the object of obsession of her number one client, Augusto (Marcello at his best). On their balconies overlooking the vibrant city below, Mara regularly chats with her neighbour, Umberto, a handsome and wholesome young man training to be a priest, rattling Mara's morals with his purity and decency. He falls for Mara, much to the objection of his disapproving Grandmother, and promises to join the foreign legion if she turns him down. Mara sets it upon herself to convince him to take up his studies at the seminary, vowing celibacy for a week if she achieves this.

Loren is superb as Mara, another turnaround from her cold and shallow creature from the preceding film. Here she is at her most lively, vivacious and gorgeous, faced with moralistic trials and challenges which threaten her way of life and idea of who she is. The famous strip tease scene, as sexy as it is believable, has gone down as the most famous and re-watched scene in Loren's career. Though it was not in the film for sensationalist reasons, it is undoubtedly sizzling, though is present to remind the viewer of the seriousness of her celibate vow.

Yesterday, Today and Tomorrow is a masterpiece of storytelling, filmmaking and performance. De Sica directs beautifully, the script flows with ease and the performances are perfection. Loren is at her finest. Though Two Women remains her most impressive and dynamic single performance, no film but this one illustrates her range and charisma. Had she made this one film alone she would forever be a legend.

Only a year after their Oscar winning triumph Yesterday, Today and Tomorrow, De Sica, Mastroianni and Loren teamed up together again for another tour de force of cinema, Marriage Italian Style, in which Loren did not play three separate characters as in the previous outing, but one woman, the role of Filumena,

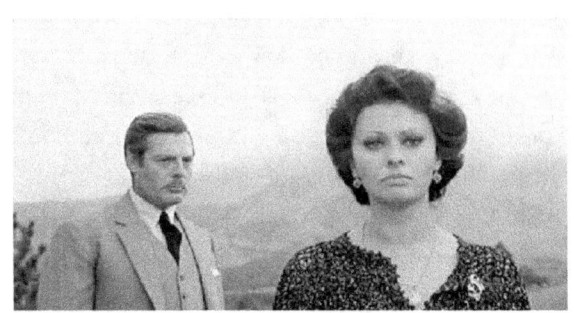

one of the most coveted parts for Italian actresses, as written by Eduardo De Filippo. Charting the life of this bold, good humoured and strong woman, Loren puts in an effort which rivals the bold characterisations of Yesterday, Today and Tomorrow and Two Women, a well rounded performance she pulls off in every area.

The film tells the story of a businessman named Domenico (Marcello Mastroianni) who meets Filumena in a brothel and moves her into his house as a mistress with the false intention that she can care for his ill mother. The film actually begins with a supposedly dying Filumena, lying in her death bed and claiming her last wish is for Domenico to marry her. However,

Domenico has met a younger woman who intends to marry, though through her careful manipulation Filumena proves more than capable of gearing the situation in her favour.

In some ways, for Loren to pull off the Filumena role was the ultimate test, a trial that if she passed would prove she was good enough to go down in history as one of the true greats. Loren later recalled that the decision for her, Ponti and De Sica to embark on an adaptation of Marriage Italian Style came when she was watching TV with her mother: "Even though after a while I started to be in movies and they were giving me already good roles, one time we were looking at the television and there was a lady called Regina Bianchi, and she was doing Marriage Italian Style. My mother, because she was very natural, sometimes she could say things that could hurt you a lot. So, I said, 'Maybe Carlo would like to do Marriage Italian Style.' And she looked at the television and she said,

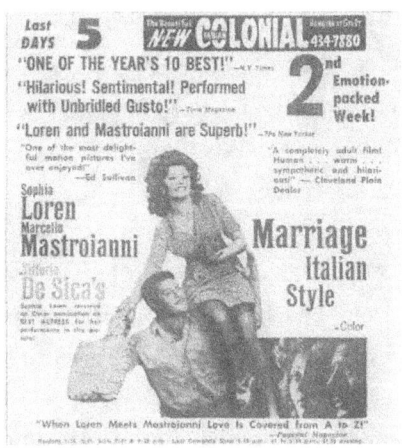

'But you could never do it.' And I said, 'Why?' 'Because she's so good.'"

Her successor may have been good, as in the words of Sophia's mother, but Loren herself is nothing short of marvellous. She embodies this multi faceted, complicated woman to a tee, from the way she walks, moves, weeps, laughs and even speaks. In every way this is a triumph. They once said Loren walking down the street was like watching Italy itself walking, and though it has become a cliché, her efforts in Marriage Italian Style seem to summarise all that is great, good and flawed about not just the kind of sassy, daring, emotional and bold woman she is portraying, but the whole nation. She is Italy embodied before our eyes.

"It's a beautiful role for a woman.," Loren later recalled. "You can cry, you can laugh, but the tragedy of the woman at that time is always there." It's vital to remember that Loren worked best when feeling as if she was in safe hands, and here she was in the hands of the masterful De Sica. Loren has often said that De Sica was the perfect director for her style of acting, "Every director has a way of showing what he wants to an actor, with words sometimes, with gestures sometimes," Loren told her son Edoardo in an on-stage interview. "For him, it was acting, from A to Z, little actors, big actors, a man, a woman. He would act the scene for everybody."

Marriage Italian Style is in the top ten films Loren ever made, a consistently engaging story directed beautifully and delicately by De Sica, while the performance she puts in is among her five greatest, hands down. Essential Loren.

81

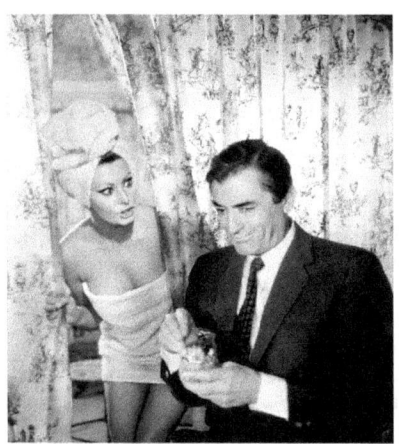

After a number of misfires and minor roles in bigger pictures, it's refreshing to come across a picture like Arabesque, which is not only a fine example of twisting and shaking up its tried and tested formula but also features a sizeable and believably portrayed role for Loren. From its swirling opening credits it is clear that Arabesque has its tongue firmly in its cheek, but its spoofy manner takes nothing away from its story, which is gripping and full of satisfying, unexpected twists.

The film begins with a professor being murdered by a man named Sloane (John Merivale) while having an eye test, who sneakily steals an Egyptian hieroglyph encoded message from the dead man's glasses. Sloane then visits Oxford Professor David Pollock, played by Gregory Peck, asking him to meet with powerful mogul Nejim Beshraavi (Alan Badel) to help with some important business. When David first declines the offer he is snatched while out running and shoved into the back of a Rolls Royce, whereupon he is convinced to assist Beshraavi in this shady matter. When David finally meets the big man, he is asked to decode the inscription on the paper Sloane stole. He then comes across Beshraavi's beautiful girlfriend, the exotic Yasmin, played by a stunning Sophia Loren. She warns him of the danger he is in and the pair develop a flirtatious fondness for one another as Pollock continues to work on the paper. Quite soon, the plot thickens, as do the complications, and Pollock finds himself in too deep to get out, tangled in a web of deception so convoluted that it would put Hitchcock to shame.

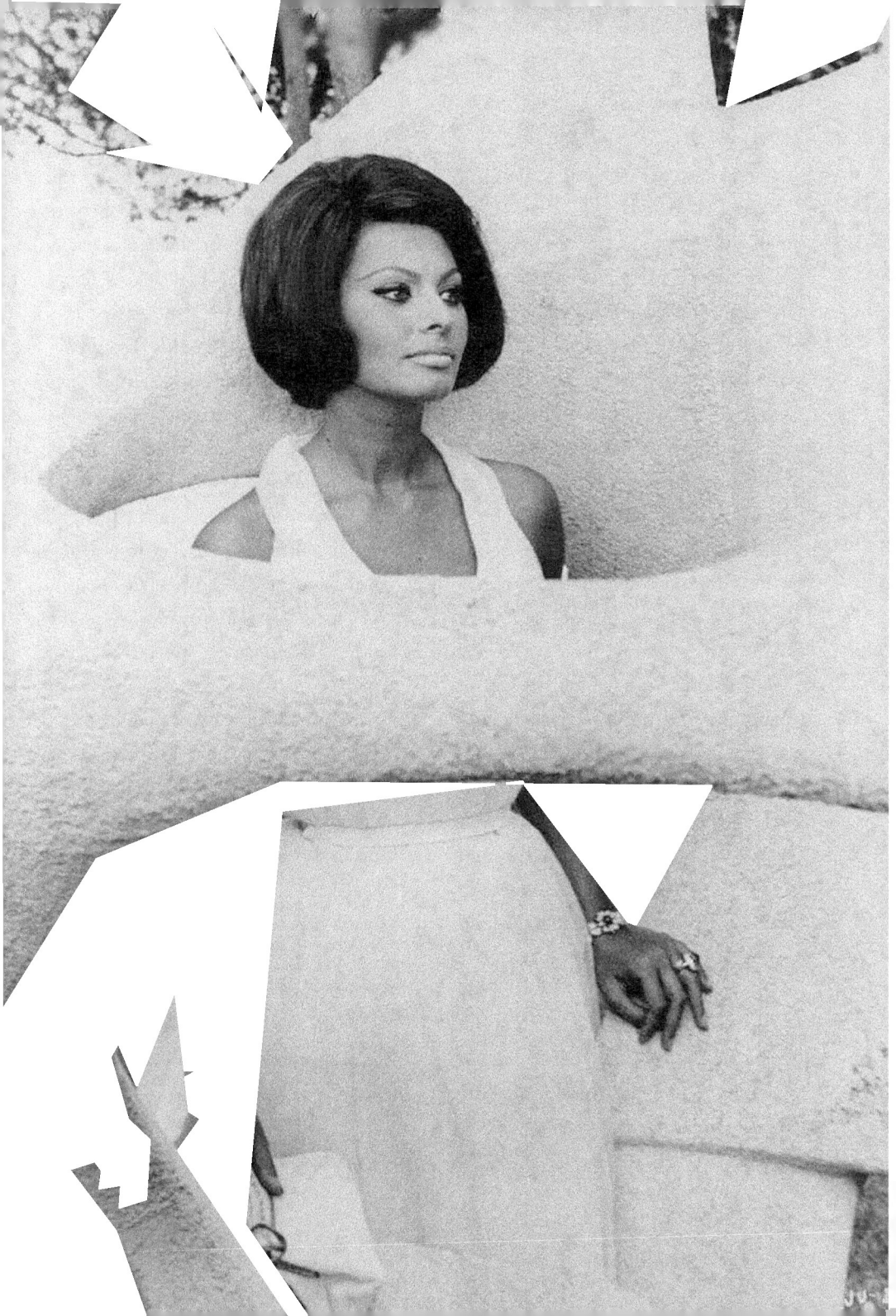

Loren is dazzling as the film's glamorous distraction in an effort than won her a Bambi Best Actress Award. Her portrayal is half comical, though underplayed enough to ensure she is still a credible female counterpart within the plot. To get under the skin of her luxurious, pampered, materialistic character, Loren demanded twenty pairs of shoes to wear through the film, hilariously prompting the script writers to make a reference to her lover's foot fetish. There is also a funny onset story about Peck not being able to keep up with Loren in the running scene, despite the fact he is supposed to be protecting her. Loren refused to slow down and asked Donen to make her co star run faster. Peck, much older than Loren and unable to keep up, was unable to do so, so thankfully for him Donen eventually convinced Loren to slow down.

Sophia Loren then got the opportunity to work with one of cinema's true greats, Charlie Chaplin. In A Countess from Hong Kong (1967) she would be directed by the great man himself, starring opposite Marlon Brando, just at the end of his first peak at this point. You could fairly apply the word underrated to a number of Chaplin movies, given that personal favourites may not receive the same amount of acclaim as some of the widely lauded masterpieces do, and opinions vary from movie to movie and person to person. But A Countess from Hong Kong is regarded by many to be one of Chaplin's weakest works, to some a slight misfire, and to others, and quite a lot it seems, an embarrassment all together. Yet upon every viewing I have found the film entertaining, warm, and though far from perfect, both charming and funny, featuring a fine farcical scenario which moves speedily so and a host of performances which are competent considering the constraints put upon the actors in question. Chaplin directs with a refreshing simplicity and though the set ups often bring to mind the static staginess of television sitcom, while

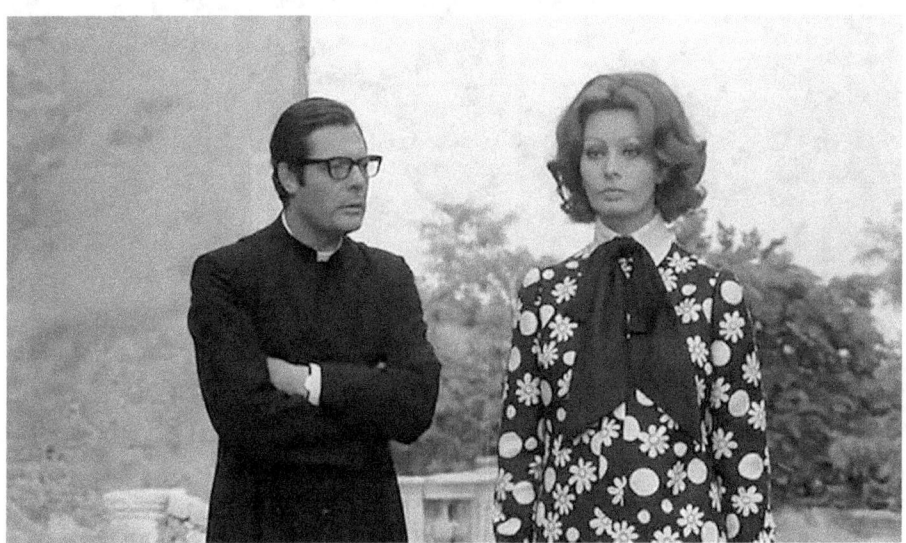

steering clear of cinematic fussiness, Charlie applies his masterly touch so well that 80 percent of it works.

The real star, for me at least, is Loren, a stunning spectacle in the middle of the slamming doors and scurried escapes, who is also very funny and effective with whatever Chaplin gives her in the film. Loren had started her decade with the very serious Two Women, but here, as she did in De Sica's finest films of the 1960s, displays her knack with comedy. In truth she is the most comfortable and effective person in the film. Unsurprisingly given her performance, Loren had a great time making the film. After all, Charlie Chaplin was one of her heroes, and she seems to have relished every second with the great man.

For the most part, as the 1970s began, it seemed that Sophia Loren had left Hollywood behind, happy with her achievements there but equally happy to semi retire from glitz-land. Though she would venture back to America for appearances and the odd film, her workload slowed down and she veered more towards her native Italy for movie roles. Much of her time was also taken up

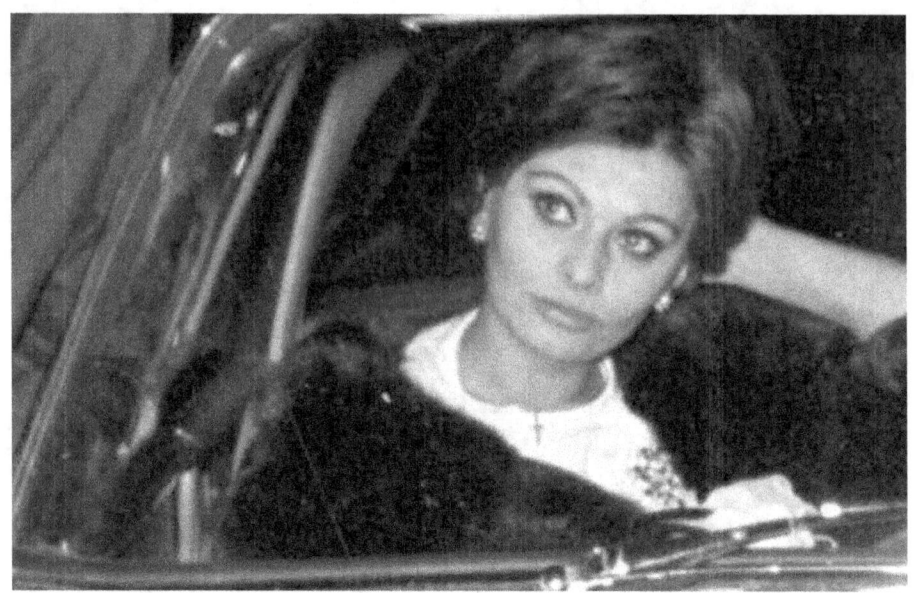

with looking after her two sons and spending time with Carlo. She did not like many of the roles offered her, so worked more selectively. Of course she did go on to make great films after this, including two gems with Mastroianni in Priest's Wife and Sunflower, not to mention their reunion in Ettore Scola's A Special Day and their final work together in Robert Altman's Pret a Porter, but it seems that Loren was more content to be a good mother, with her days as a Hollywood megastar fondly remembered in the past.

The exciting news is of course that Netflix are releasing a new film featuring Loren in the lead role, The Life Ahead. At the age of 85, though she's been away from full length features for a decade, it's clear that Sophia is far from done just yet.

Speaking to the Guardian recently, Loren said "I say to myself: 'Shut up. Be strong. Just keep going and try. Sometimes you make mistakes and sometimes you win.' I made some mistakes... But still I won."

END.

WORLD CINEMA ICON
THEO ANGELOPOULOS

"What is important, what has meaning, is the journey... and journeys are through history as well as through a landscape."

The films of Theodoros Angelopoulos are among the most striking, poetic and beautiful in the history of cinema. Certainly an acquired taste, even for those attuned to the often slower rhythms and irregular narrative structures of world cinema, they are meditative works haunted by Greece's turbulent history, the past being very present in the eyes of Theo's protagonists. If one does have the patience for his style of slow, careful, but paradoxically complex film (and I hope anyone reading this does) then his work can be thoroughly rewarding. Vitally though, Theo's films cannot and should not be watched casually, but studied, viewed multiple times and taken in with care.

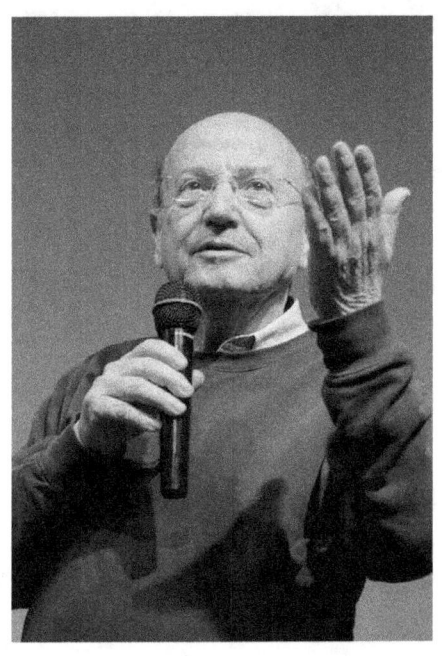

Harvey Keitel, who was cast in Theo's 1995 masterpiece Ulysses' Gaze, once made a joke that if you were to sit down in the cinema for one of Angelopoulos's films, you could go out for popcorn, come back five minutes later and see it was still on the same shot. Though partly true, viewers would be wise to stick around, for even one of his most stationery camera set ups usually reveals a detail so fine that once it becomes clear, usually by the subtle arrival of a figure or a tiny shift of the camera, it hits you more directly than a frantic camera movement ever could. His framing, use of slow zoom and expertise with stillness is hypnotic to say the least, and his films never fail to pull me in from their first scene onwards.

Martin Scorsese, a connoisseur of cinema if there ever was one, described him as "a masterful filmmaker. He really understands how to control the frame. There are sequences in his work—the wedding scene in The Suspended Step of the Stork; the rape scene in Landscape in the Mist; or any given scene in The Travelling Players—where the slightest movement, the slightest change in distance, sends reverberations through the film and through the viewer. The total effect is hypnotic, sweeping, and profoundly emotional. His sense of control is almost otherworldly."

Angelopoulos' style of filmmaking could be traced back to his childhood, especially when one considers the static, melancholic mood of his films. He was born in Athens in April of 1935, and it was during the Greek Civil War that his father was kidnapped and taken prisoner. Theo said it was when waiting for his father to return, his absence which was very much apparent, and even searching for his body amongst the dead, that directly inspired his film work. This would literally have an impact on films like Landscape in the Mist (1988), about two children looking for their father, travelling from Greece to Germany in an epic odyssey, but it would also inspire the whole atmosphere and pensiveness of his cinema. "This happened in December 1944," he said in 2009, "the so called red December in Athens, during the battle between the right and left in which my father was arrested. He was then led outside Athens somewhere near Peristeri where he was going to be executed. As a nine year old boy, I remember

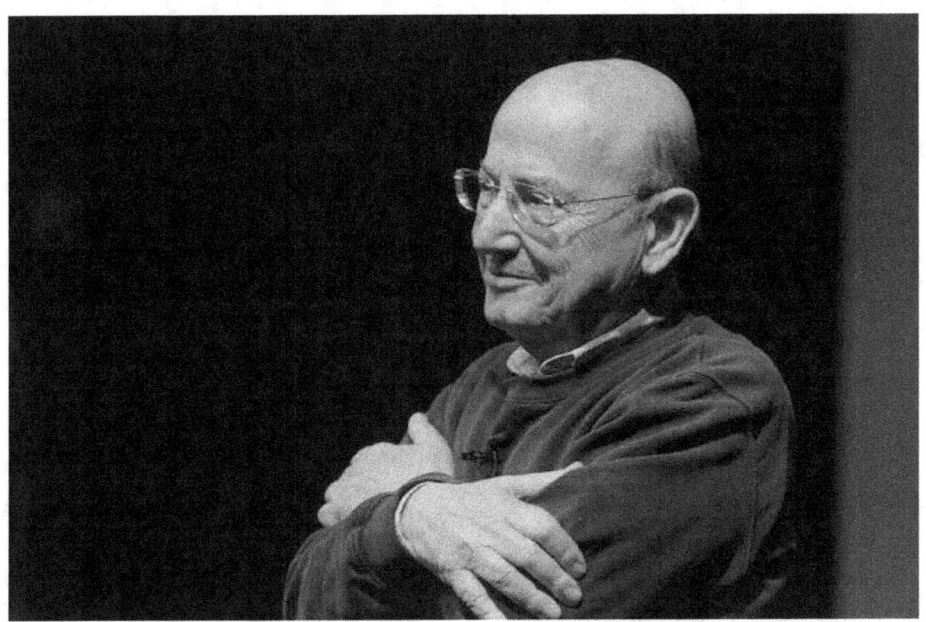

wandering around the outskirts of the city, in the fields, with my mother among the many dead bodies lying around, looking for my father."

Prior to his filmmaking "career" (for want of a better word), Theo studied law at the University of Athens before taking part in his military service and briefly attending the Sorbonne in Paris. He then made further studies in film before heading back home to Greece to pursue cinema, starting off with shorts in the late sixties before moving on to his politically motivated feature films. His individualistic style came about almost immediately, sprawling films lacking in traditional film story telling techniques, characterised by long, careful camera movements which were often much more complex than met the eye. Though political in their tone, Theo's films were ultimately about humanity, the fatality of detachment, the inevitability of alienation and the tragedy of Greece's history - and of course its present day, irremovable from its legacy. Theo was drawn to journeys, adventures that stretched long across the landscape but further into the soul; modern Greek tragedies if you will. These epic odysseys were made all the more poetic and poignant because quite often there was nothing at the end of the pursuit. Theo was concerned, if not obsessed and frustrated, with the rigidity of Greece's borders, the ramifications of immigration and the concept of uprooting ones' meagre belongings, the physical body, and most importantly the soul. Separation, segregation and categorising human beings, using them as play things for politics, also became fixtures of his work.

When considering Angelopoulos's films it is hard if not impossible to find a director with whom he can be compared. Of course, when experiencing one of his films (indeed, experiencing is the best word one could use), looking for similarities and contemporaries is the last thing on your mind, for one is too immersed in the visuals and atmosphere to ponder on such matters. But it is afterwards, when the film haunts you the most, that you realise what a singular talent he really was. Literally no one made a film like Theo Angelopoulos. Though he often admitted Orson Welles was his only true influence (mainly on a technical level, for it is clear that Welles' often exaggerated, cartoonish style could not be further from Theo's), spiritually and aesthetically he had no equal. The emotion in his films, almost always hidden and suppressed, also makes him singular.

When Theo died in a car crash in January of 2012, aged 76, he had been working on his 14th picture. The fact that we only have 13 Theo Angelopoulos films to pour over seems a shame (true, there are also shorts and documentaries), but then Theo took his time with his films, preparing every shot like a grand composition, establishing a mood for each picture and never faltering from it. From his earliest films like

Reconstruction (1970), The Travelling Players (1975) and The Hunters (1977) he dispensed with familiar film rhythms, the usual character development and pacing, by establishing his own mode of story telling that was both hopelessly grim and compulsively addictive viewing. With every film, every scene, every shot (sometimes the scene only has one shot of course), Angelopoulos cast a spell on his viewer, a kind of hypnotism that ensured you were with his central character from the first frame to the last.

As the years went on his films became even more haunting. They were searches for inner and outer peace that rarely, if ever, resulted in what Hollywood movie goers might call a happy ending. But Theo's films were not interested in ticking boxes and following formulas. They told more in a silence, in a figure standing alone in some bleak street or foggy field than a whole blockbuster could in its whole bombastic 90 minutes.

Theo also attracted some big names to his meditative cinema; he worked twice with Marcello Mastroianni, firstly on the masterpiece The Beekeeper (1986) and again on the enigmatic The Suspended Step of the Stork (1991). He also worked with Harvey Keitel on the Cannes Grand Jury Prize winner Ulysses' Gaze (1995), one of Angelopoulos's most mesmerising films.

Angelopoulos had the opportunity to leave Greece and make films abroad. But he wanted to stay at home, basically in a quest to try and answer the big question, "why?", and face his country's complex, tragic but poetic history. He once said, "It's not only that the civil war is not presented as part of history, but I have the impression that the same is true for many of the vital moments in the history of this country; there is a systematic attempt to exclude them from the official history that is being taught in the schools. There are taboo subjects. So unless there is a proper dialogue over Greek history, to bring together the present and the past, we will never be able to 'read' the present and to understand what the future can entail."

Was it his goal to ensure the past was not kept as a distant ghost, but as a part of everyone's current situation? The heavy sadness of Greek history haunts most of his films, and his characters seem to be carrying the weight of it. His work may not be fun, stylish or quotable (clearly they are far from shallow or superficial works), but it is hugely important in ensuring mankind does not forget what has already been. Hitchcock once said that self plagiarism was style, and though Theo was no flash director, he did have a style that was very much his own, a cinematic voice impossible to replicate.

Despite his bleak view, Angelopoulos was also hopeful that his country, and indeed the world, could recover: "I belong to an older generation, a generation that believed that change was possible, that it was possible to change the world, that it was possible to open up a new path. My generation believed that it was possible not only to dream of a new world, but also to turn dreams into realities. It didn't happen. I think we are all carrying the shadow of disappointment and failure. Yet, in spite this, and contrary to what pessimists and nay-sayers believe, I believe that history moves about in a meandering way, sometimes going up and sometimes going down. Right now we are in a downturn, but there will be an upturn eventually."

THE BEEKEEPER (1986)

"In The Beekeeper, alienation and despair have so metastasized in the film's central figure that he's virtually one of the walking dead."
- The Beekeeper synopsis on Theo Angelopoulos' website

The Beekeeper, the second film in Theo's "trilogy of silence" (the first part was 1984's Voyage to Cythera) is a careful, precise work which grabs you from its first stark image and keeps you hooked until the very end.

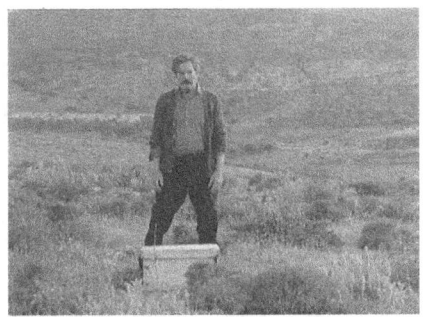

Though steered by controlled yet emotive performances, it is a film driven by Angelopoulos' directorial grace, ensuring every scene and shot is assured and applied with care, thus hypnotising the viewer. Quite how Theo achieves this, with little dialogue, such slow movements and often bleak surroundings, is a testament to his brilliance. Though some might ignorantly call it more of the same, another typically pensive Angelopoulos portrait of alienation and displacement, this time self inflicted, there are subtle difference with The Beekeeper to the rest of his filmography.

The Beekeeper, often unfairly overlooked in his oeuvre, stars Marcello Mastroianni as Spyros, a teacher just giving up his post at a school to take off on the road with his van full of bees for their yearly ritual. We first encounter him at the wedding of his daughter, where we learn there have been complications in the family which have caused a rift. Unhappy amongst the gathered revellers, he poses awkwardly for the family group shot and wanders the house alone as they laugh and drink down stairs. After the strained ceremony, Spyros slopes off and begins his journey. Dissatisfied with his life and family, Spyros leaves his wife behind. He is detached from his surroundings, only happy when seeing to his bees for their annual honey trip, taking them from place to place, and being completely absorbed in the task.

One day he picks up a female hitchhiker, played by Nadia Mourouzi, a young drifter who has lost her way. Though they speak very little, the girl feels a connection to Spyros and sticks to him as much as she can. When he sets down in his lodgings in a tiny Greek town, without speaking she follows him inside. Both settling down on a single bed each, the pair drift to sleep, though Spyros is angered when she brings back a young soldier and has sex with him, loudly, in the middle of the night., Ordering her to pack her bags, Spyros tries to shake her off. Yet something keeps bringing them together and after he tries to ditch her, he finds her pull too much to resist somehow. After visiting his wife one last time to say goodbye, Spyros finds the girl sitting in a cafe. In one of the film's most shocking moments he drives his van into the cafe window and the girl, though stunned, instinctively jumps in the passenger seat and re joins her friend on the road.

These two lonely lost souls stick together. On a boat trip Spyros tries to have sex with her, roughly and clumsily, but she fights him off and objects to his forcefulness, saying 'Not like this' and clearly hoping for a more fitting if not perfect moment for their bodies to meet. Eventually they come to a run down row of buildings by a railroad track and enter an abandoned cinema owned by Spyros's old friend. It is about to be closed down and the kind old man working the projector allows them to sleep on the stage beneath the projector screen. In a passionate, overwhelming scene, the pair have contorted, almost animalistic sex, but after their physical merging, which was a long time coming, things are never the same. They go for a walk in the town, disconnected from one another. They attempt to have dinner in a small restaurant but the girl knows it is all wrong and that their union is doomed. "Let me go", she says. She storms out, he follows and they enjoy one last embrace before she retrieves her belongings from the cinema, leaving Spyros standing by the tracks, alone and pensive.

Later he heads to a field with his bees, where in a rage he lets off all the lids and succumbs to a death by multiple bee-sting. The final shot is of his hand, as the life leaves his twitching body, before the camera zooms up to the blue sky, infested by the frantic buzzing of the bees Spyros

94

had been dedicating so much time to. In short, he becomes their sacrifice.

In my view, The Beekeeper is one of the finest films in the history of Greek cinema, and for me among the most effective and affecting films of the 1980s. Though unfairly sidelined in the era of the blockbuster when the art film was in submission, this downbeat but strangely compulsive film is consistently engaging, due largely to Theo's imaginative and unusual camera movements and techniques. He is also aided by Marcello Mastroianni, delivering the subtlest and perhaps most devastating performance of his career. Spyros is a mysterious figure, who says very little in words but speaks volumes in his detached demeanour and slow, careful movements. He is not a likeable man, but we find that we begin to care for him, despite his shortcomings. It is clear from the wedding scene that he is not a great father to say the least, a man who wants to escape his past but simply cannot, and is equally as dissatisfied with his present. Not only is he stuck in the past but he is tormented by it, a cold man whose eyes say nothing on the surface but reveal hidden depths as the film goes on. His is a wasted life.

Nadia is bewitching also, an enigmatic girl who first appears to be free but is in fact as lost as can be. She clings to the old man like a child to a disinterested father, admitting that he is the only person who has ever been kind to her. Yet she still teases him, like the spoilt brat who does not appreciate true kindness. He at first tries to brush her off, but finds his obsession intensifying. Only when he says a final so long to his wife can he pursue the girl and this doomed future. He is ageing, has seen better days and is unable to face up to the facts. The bees offer him a goal, a purpose, and the girl promises new horizons. In reality, neither bring him anything of lasting worth.

There is an aspect to The Beekeeper which falls out of Theo's control, and may in fact be just a case of this viewer looking too closely. Throughout the film, Mastroianni seems to carry his own cinematic legacy around with him, and though he could not be more different here than in his earlier famous roles, his iconic status seems strangely apparent behind the anonymous moustached face of Spyros. In the scene when he and the girl sleep beneath the blank cinema screen, Marcello seems to address his past directly; and seeing as the cinema itself is closing down, he even seems to be lamenting the decline of cinema (Marcello did it more directly in 1989's Splendor, where he played the manager of an ailing small town cinema) while referencing his own illustrious past and intimidating career on screen. On set, his co star was extremely nervous about working with Marcello, especially when considering his legendary status. But he soon calmed her down by spending time relaxing and drinking with her, so they could work together more freely, spared of his legacy and stature. Still, his iconic legacy haunts the film and Spyros's demeanour throughout.

Theo seems intent on establishing Spyros as a man without prospects, a doomed figure in a doomed land. One of the saddest scenes, one proving that Spyros is a man stuck in the creases of time, is when he and two old friends - one of whom he has snuck out of a hospital - go and drink wine on a beach in an attempt to recapture the glorious freedom of their youths. The ailing friend dances before the sea, while the other, a rich business man equally disenfranchised with his lot, strips naked and runs fearlessly into the water. Even in this scenario, Spyros is dissatisfied, seeing the sad truth and the rather pathetic fates of he and his old comrades.

Yet it is the girl, never named, who gives the film its real dramatic impact and in Spyros ignites a hint of life. There is a strange tension in their relationship, with him paradoxically seeing her as both an object of desire and rebellious daughter. On the other end, she sees him both as a father and a rock, though is aware of the doomed fate of their union. They are drawn to one another but remain detached, a fact which is repeated in the visuals and camera choices of Theo.

One of the key moments between the pair comes when the girl is leaning off a refreshment van while he goes to find a building he once called home, which has, of course, been abandoned and left to ruin. While there he recalls a song he would sing to his daughter, long ago when days were brighter. He returns to see the girl drunk at the stand. In a slow zoom beginning from around fifty metres away, Theo comes in close to observe the strange paring, and the grizzly details when the girl bites Spyros's hand, drawing blood. It's a disturbing scene and highlights the toxicity of this duo.

What is most striking about The Beekeeper is how it prefers the importance of body language and imagery over dialogue. Subtlety is not quite the word; Theo's use of camera techniques invites the kind of careful minimalism which may exhaust fans of Hollywood blockbusters but please anyone drawn to a true and believable human story. It's a film where every brush stroke is applied with care, from the nuanced performances, the bleak but strangely comforting locations, to the precise choices of angles, zooms and framing. It is pure cinema; not merely "pictures of people talking" as Alfred Hitchcock dubbed the modern and often uncinematic film style, but a movie of evocative images.

Unfortunately The Beekeeper did not set the world alight, though Theo probably knew it was not going to be a money spinner, nor did he set out to make it - or any other film for that matter - for the box office takings. Reviewers at the time seemed to miss the point and didn't have the patience for the delicacy of Theo's vision. Janet Maslin in the New York Times said it wasted Marcello's talents, and wrote that "not even those inclined to dwell on the film's occasional honeycomb imagery or its heavy sense of foreboding will find much to command the attention."

Time Out were even less impressed, writing in their small minded review, "Angelopoulos' odyssey of a middle-aged man in the grip of terminal emptiness has a stately pace and a shortage of event or information that are a lot to take. It's always raining, usually evening, and the settings are mainly petrol stations and sad rooming houses in Greek tank towns. Spyros remains uncomplaining, wordless and lifeless throughout. They finally get it on in a neglected cinema, which not only fails to buck up his ideas, but appears to confirm his disenchantment, because the next day he surrenders to death by bee-sting. A muffled, deeply interior film."

Retrospectively however, the film has made new fans and contemporary reviews reveal more understanding. When the film was re-released on DVD in 2010, the Independent wrote "the film is tender but tough-going, its air of melancholy beginning with a grim wedding scene and not letting up till the inevitable conclusion. The beekeeper's journey leads him away from strained family relations and into a new, but equally fraught, interaction with a young, cheekily charming hitchhiker. There's an ambiguous sexual charge in the air, and The Beekeeper includes some extremely uncomfortable scenes as Angelopoulos pushes at the boundaries of the relationship. But the directing is assured, and the performances restrained and heartbreakingly believable."

Rob Batchelor wrote a positive appreciation of the film for the website Roobla in 2010: "Some viewers might baulk at slow, depressing Greek cinema, but for fans of beautiful images and uncomfortable, frustratingly uncommunicative characters... The Beekeeper could be the perfect film. Consider it the anti-My Big Fat Greek Wedding."

In his book, A Short Chronology of World Cinema, Dennis Grunes wrote of the film: "O melissokomos, from Greece, Italy and France, is a mostly silent, sleepy piece saturated with the honey of melancholy. It is pure ache, and a reminder of how penetrating an artist Angelopoulos could be. Fleetingly reminiscent of late Visconti, some of it wears a bit thin; but most of it deeply moved this viewer with its sense of a cultural and cross-cultural abandonment of vivid feeling. In this context, the girl, drunk, draws blood by biting Spyros's wrist. It is a perilous rush for all of us."

The Beekeeper is a rare treasure, a restrained, often harrowing but perversely relaxing film which reveals truths in mere zooms and camera pulls, taking these two tragic figures to places few filmmakers would think of, or even dare to go. In the hands of a lesser talent, The Beekeeper could have easily been clichéd, a predictable case of girl-meets-older-man/father-figure, with the pair falling in love despite the sea of differences. In Theo's hands however, it is a hopelessly sad, dirty, gritty, unflinching depiction of what might happen if two very different people were drawn together in a bleak and unforgiving landscape which offers them no salvation as a duo or lone crusaders.

Theo himself called it a film about "the conflict between memory and non memory". Again, though involved in deep character study, he is clearly making a film about modern Greece, as seen through the sad eyes of Spyros. Like the protagonist's soul, Theo's mid 80s Greece is broken and crumbling. His choices of towns reflect this, as do the buildings he focuses on, simultaneously beautiful and shoddy, the bricks crumbling even as the ornate tiled patterns and door frames remain mostly intact, like ghosts from the past still haunting long after their time is up.

In his book on Angelopoulos' films, Andrew Horton said The Beekeeper was Theo's cinematic reaction to the suicide of Nikos Poulantzas in 1979, though there does not seem to be any documented proof that this was the case. It was however, by Theo's admission, a film which marked his shift from more politically minded films to ones concerned with humanity. Even if one chooses not to see Theo's film as a depiction of his homeland, damaged as it is, one can at least view it as a story of two people experiencing extreme suppression and tension. Though the girl is potential company for the old man, she is in fact physical proof of his desperate loneliness and isolation in a world he has fallen out of love with. In the end, there is only one place to go. Marcello's performance is a tour de force, absolutely flawless, and he never puts a single foot wrong in his journey to his sad realisation. He worked with Theo again on The Suspended Step of the Stork, perhaps just as effectively. Here though, in nearly every scene and very much the focal point of Angelopoulos' investigations, they work together as one, united in their aims.

Marcello himself loved the experience of making The Beekeeper. He recalled the challenge of being stung by the bees. "We had to repeat the scene for three days running," said Marcello. "Somebody said to me, Why do you bother taking such risks? But we were in Greece, not Hollywood, where you can make bees with a remote control. You just had to go for it. It was a beautiful experience, a hard film though, because there is not much urban development in Greece. In the end I did my own dubbing in Greek. We worked for months."

Speaking in the late 1990s, Angelopoulos stated, "Some films have at their origins an intellectual premise. In others, it is sentiment. For instance, The Hunters was almost entirely conceived intellectually. The same for Days of '36. The Beekeeper comes straight from the heart. Most of my films are in-between, a combination of both."

Indeed, The Beekeeper seems less on the intellectual side and much more personal and straight forward. How much of Angelpopoulos there is in Spyros though, we may never know.

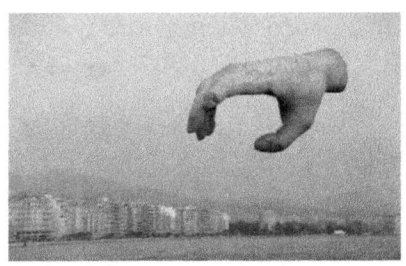

LANDSCAPE IN THE MIST
(1988)

The third film in Theo Angelopoulos's Trilogy of Silence is Landscape in the Mist, which is also widely regarded (and I believe rightly so) to be one of his finest pieces of work. Like The Beekeeper before it (and indeed The Suspended Step of the Stork which would emerge three years later as the first instalment in his Trilogy of Borders) it is another epic odyssey, only this one focuses, rather unusually I might add, on the quest of two young children, a brother and sister, who are heading out on a voyage to locate their absent father.

Tania Palailogou plays Voula, a young girl who lives with her mother (an elusive presence in the picture) and five year old brother Alexandro, played by the brilliant Michalis Zeke. Having never met their father, and curious to do so, they have been told that he left Greece for Germany years earlier. Though it was undoubtedly a ruse to ensure they lost interest in a man who clearly did not care, the pair head out of the family home (though calling it a family home is perhaps an overstatement) for Germany, in a naive bid to see their dad. Their first attempt however goes wrong. When they arrive at Athens Railway Station, they are spotted by a police man who takes them to an uncle they know very little. He insists they have no father in Germany and that they in fact both have different dads and are products of their mother's one night stands. Even though the children over hear this revelation, they still believe their mother's version of the story, and are not going to give up. They are Germany bound.

Along the way, as the weather and landscape becomes cold and unforgiving, they encounter the driver of a group of travelling actors, Orestis (Stratos Tzortzoglou) who takes them some way of their journey but cannot get them the whole way there. They then come across a truck driver, who though initially kind to them, goes on to rape Voula. In that instant she is no longer a little girl but a refugee of humanity, in one act robbed of her childhood and forced to face the harsh reality of life. Later they come across Orestis again, a kind face willing to help. Still, they are restless in their pursuit for Germany and the father they insist is waiting for their arrival.

Ultimately a modern Greek tragedy, Landscape in the Mist is one of the most striking pictures of the 80s, if not of the whole 20th century. With a constant air of sadness, there is a beauty on the hope the children carry with them, the determination they have to meet their father. The two young leads are tremendously good, Tania Palaiologou embodying quite brilliantly a young girl who was previously unaware that there are bad people out in the world ready to take advantage and steal her youth; young Michalis Zeke, the very face of innocence, is also brilliant, a natural actor who is able to convey the wide eyed naivety of a five year old.

Though the landscape Theo refers to is the unreachable location, and the father is the unobtainable figure unseen to their eyes but alive in their hearts, it is their quest itself which becomes the film's main preoccupation. The goal is enigmatic simply because we know as viewers that it does not exist, but their adventures along the way are what they really learn from, regardless of the fact that their odyssey is one without a true goal.

Theo's filmography is full of unforgettable sequences to rival the best in cinema history, but Landscape in the Mist seems to have more than any other; early on for instance, the scene in which the two children inform the inmates of a bleak mental institution, in particular a man they refer to as bird (vitally trying to fly over the mesh fence which separates him from freedom), that they are heading for Germany, is utterly haunting, especially when one observes the longing in the man's eyes when he learns of their impending journey. A similarly striking scene, only much more disturbing, is when the children are in the snowy small town and come across the horse which comes loose off a rope in the middle of the road after being dragged along by a car; the boy, weeping, is horrified to watch it die before his eyes. It also features two other very poignant sequences; one is when the children see a large sculpture of a pointing hand being lifted from the ocean and then, symbolically of course, watch the finger come loose and back into the sea, highlighting the aimlessness of their journey (and of course, of Greece as a country at that moment in time, lost without true guidance). Perhaps the most disturbing, upsetting and unsettling scene is when young Voula is raped. We do not, thankfully of course, see any of the rape, but the man taking her into the back of the van, which in some ways is more unnerving. Knowing what is happening, as her younger brother sleeps soundly in the passenger seat, we observe the scene in total silence, the camera not moving once, and only beginning a slow zoom when the rapist flees the van and we are shown, subtly, some blood on the wall of the vehicle. Martin Scorsese later picked it out as one of the most remarkable scenes of modern cinema, and even now, some thirty odd years on it remains unforgettable and harrowing in equal measure.

Angelopoulos himself was first inspired to make the film by a newspaper article which told of two children going out on a similar quest, as in his film, to find their father in Germany. The image of these two small figures, on the look out for someone and indeed something they couldn't hope to find, stuck with him and directly gave birth to Landscape in the Mist. But Angelopoulos insisted it wasn't "just about two children looking for their father. It is a journey which is the initiation into life. On the road they learn everything—love and death, lies and truth, beauty and destruction. The journey is simply a way to focus on what life gives us all."

Co written with Thanassis Valtinos and Tonino Guerra, it reminds one of L'Avventura, the iconic Antonioni film which Guerra himself had a hand in writing. Though they vary in many ways, both films are quests, journeys, with characters searching for an object which not only eludes them but also proves impossible to find; in Angelopoulos's film it's the father, in L'Avventura it's the friend who went missing at sea on a yacht. Like Antonioni's own film, Landscape in the Mist is bleak, devoid of humour and at times relentlessly painful viewing. Yet it is also full of beauty, dark beauty of course, but the visuals and poetics stop it from being a hopelessly depressing picture. After all, there is positivity in the hope of the children, however misguided and naive it may be.

Speaking of his writing relationship with Guerra, Angelopoulos told Dan Fainaru in 1999: "It is true we do not need to speak the same language, but we are both men of the South. I believe that all the Mediterranean people have something in common. Not only because there are ancient roots common to all of us, having been in contact with each other for thousands of years, but also because of the proximity of the sea and the similitude of the climate. I never feel abroad when I am in Italy. We immediately realized we were speaking the same language – in film terms of course, because when we met I spoke French and he spoke Italian but we understood each other perfectly. We also discovered there are many things for which we share the same affection and love. What I like about Tonino is not only the fact that he is a poet, but also that earthly, peasant side, which for me, is very important."

"I must first explain that while basically, I am the author of my own scripts, I always need another person who will play the devil's advocate, the psychoanalyst or whatever, to give me a different perspective of the things I have in mind. He is to be the first person to hear my ideas in the raw, and his feedback helps me choose the right direction. In the case of Tonino, most of the time he acts the part of the psychoanalyst. I am not sure many people work together the way we do. Once a film is finished and I feel I am ready to start the next one, I go to his village in the mountains. We sit down, talk about everything and anything, have a drink, and then go to lunch. Later, as we sit down and relax, he will ask me whether I have anything in mind I would like to work on. At this point I am still doubtful. I start talking, telling him different stories I had been reflecting upon, ideas that caught my fancy, images that stuck in my mind, nothing yet very organized one way or another. I am walking back and forth; he listens to me, sitting down. When there is something he considers to be of particular interest, he stops me and writes it down..."

Not only are the children lost, but so is everyone else in the film. The locations Theo chooses are similarly bleak and battered, highlighting that these lost people exist in a lost land. It is also a film haunted by Greek's past; this is illustrated when the travelling actors (all of whom are a reference to Theo's earlier picture, The Travelling Players) stand on a suitably desolate beach recalling war time memories, of both the Greek Civil War and the Second World War. It's a very direct reference of course, but Theo is often at his best when his symbolism is more obvious and easy to decipher.

Upon release, Theo's film achieved wide acclaim, being hailed as perhaps the finest film he had made up to that point, and it also earned numerous honours across the globe, such as the Silver Lion at the Venice Film Festival, a prestigious gong at the Berlin International Film Festival, as well as Best Film at the European Film Awards and a nomination for

Best Foreign Language Film at the Oscars.

It could be argued that Angelopoulos's work, and this film in particular, if not celebrates alienation but at least presents it in a romantic fashion. He, like some viewers, may feel strangely soothed by the melancholic mood of his pictures, yet even when it all threatens to get too much, he presents it with such beauty and care that the blackness never truly overtakes his aim or the aesthetic and poetic poignancy of the film. To some of course, perhaps those more attuned to Hollywood action and American pacing, Landscape in the Mist will be the most doom laden film in the world. After all, the Greece depicted here is not the one the tourists will see, but the "other Greece" which Theo was committed to portraying throughout his career as a filmmaker.

At the centre of the film though is the literal search for a father. Theo admitted that many of his films feature such a search, and one only has to look through to see his filmography to see that fact; from his debut, Recreation, to The Beekeeper and beyond. Here though, this longing desire for a father is more literal, and in looking for their dad the children, especially the girl, find more out about themselves and the world at large, even if their father remains elusive.

Theo saw all his films as odysseys, and he also saw them as road movies with a difference: "Usually, in road movies, the characters roam from one place to another without a definite purpose. In my films, these journeys always have a goal. In *Voyage to Cythera*, for instance, it is the journey to the imaginary island of one's dreams, the island of peace and happiness. In *Landscape in the Mist* the children are looking for their father. The reporter in *The Suspended Step of the Stork* is travelling around for a definite reason; he is trying to unveil the mystery of the politician who disappeared. In *Ulysses' Gaze* the entire trip through the Balkans is determined by the wish to find some pieces of lost film."

Reviews at the time saw Theo elevated to the status of a cinema master. The New York Times dubbed it a crime that he wasn't better known, and held his film up as a masterpiece, though they did criticise his often blunt symbolism.

Writing years later on Roger Ebert's website, Wael Khairy called it a "work of art that comes from the feelings, dreams, sorrows and flashes of life that we experience every day. I find myself thinking about these children time and time again as I go through my own journey in life... Once seen it will never be forgotten."

Though the film does end, Theo has often said that none of his films truly finish and each one thematically leads into the next one he will make. "This is the reason you will never find the word 'End' at the end of any of my films. As far as I am concerned, these are chapters of one and the same film that goes on and will never be finished, for there is never a final word on anything. I believe we never manage to do more than a fraction of the things we'd like to do."

Though the children embrace the tree at the end of their overnight boat trip at the film's climax, one does not sense the book is closed. Indeed, the children's arduous quest is not truly over, and perhaps never will be.

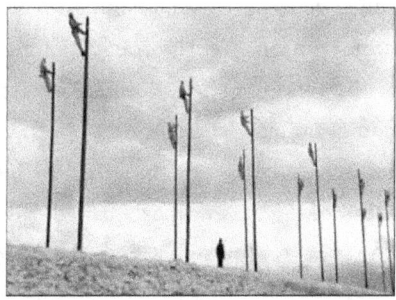

THE SUSPENDED STEP OF THE STORK (1991)

Five years on from the release of The Beekeeper, world cinema icon Marcello Mastroianni signed up to work with Theo Angelopoulos once again for The Suspended Step of the Stork, another startling and meditative piece from the master of understatement. Strangely soothing in its considered motions, though to some an undoubtedly bleak piece of work, it is a political film through and through, never blatant in its directives but sure of itself, in all its symbolism, as a statement on border control and the very ludicrous nature of borders on a basic level.

In the film, Gregory Karr plays a reporter on the bordering town which separates Greece and Albania, documenting the rigorous struggles of the refugees stuck there. However, photographing the plights of others for so long, with the aid of his filmmaking team, has turned him into an almost robotic being, incapable of empathy and feeling but always looking for the good shot amidst genuine suffering. At one point in the film, when very aware and rather tired of the trapped existence he shares with the refugees in the grim town, he shouts out, in a fit of frustration, that all he knows to be is a filmmaker, but he's one without compassion who never thinks of his subject's feelings. While filming with his crew, he becomes obsessed with an older gentleman who sells potatoes in the town (Marcello Mastroianni), and quickly becomes convinced he is in fact a famous politician who disappeared a number of years earlier. The reporter contacts the MPs wife, played by Jeanne Moreau, inviting her to the town to identify him. The resulting film charts the reporter's journey and investigation, though his quest for the truth, both within himself and in regards to the true identity of the potato seller, seem secondary to the plight of the people of the town who have found themselves stuck between the seams of society.

Angelopoulos is at his best here, choreographing masterful scenes that border on the balletic, breathtaking as they are in their graceful delicacy. Quite how he achieved the heights he reaches here is beyond thought, and Theo, one might say, is the true star of his own movies. That said, the acting from the three main players is just as impressive. Karr makes for a solid lead, the emotionless man lost in a strange dream, existing on borders as if in some kind of detached limbo. While some reviewers did criticise Karr's performance as being dull and lifeless, such traits work in favour of this disenfranchised man, looking for humanity in a land that inspires the visionary in him but leaves him incapable of assessing his true emotions. Mastroianni is at his most restrained, as he was in The Beekeeper of course, here as a man who may or may not be this mythical politician. It's a sturdy, dedicated feat of acting, keeping the viewer at bay and at a distance at all times, to retain the mystique of this enigmatic individual. Once again, he does not put a foot wrong. Moreau, Marcello's co star from Antonioni's La Notte, puts in a similarly effective and understated effort, but each cast member is a slave (albeit willing slaves) to Theo's vision. Moreau has some particularly strong scenes early on in the movie; firstly at the posh house party where she is interrupted by Karr who informs her of his decision to find her husband; secondly, in and outside Karr's

apartment, where she recalls her final night with her husband before he vanished, recalling with tears when they made love like strangers in the darkness. Moreau is extraordinary here, but what is more extraordinary is how Angelopoulos restrains himself from going into close up. In fact that whole scene, as long as it is, is all in one take, making Moreau's performance in that instant all the more marvellous. Still, the scene also hits the spot because there is no clichéd backing music to heighten the emotion, nor the kind of camera trickery which manipulates emotions from viewers of Hollywood pictures. None of this is needed, for Angelopoulos' paradoxically distant and intimate camera technique aids Moreau's naked emotion and ensures the viewer feels like a curious onlooker rather than an intruder.

Angelopoulos doesn't always get his due credit as the master he truly was, and understandably some people do not have the patience for his brand of hypnotic, often largely silent cinema. Yet some of the sequences here I would rank alongside the most powerful in the history of the filmed image; the tracking shot of the train carriages for instance, each filled with a face as hopelessly lost as the last one, is stunning; similarly, the shot of Marcello smoking outside his lodgings, seen in a slow zoom before he throws away the butt of the cigarette, is also mesmerising; the traditional Greek wedding scene, where the occasion is performed in almost complete silence with the families standing on opposing sides of the river which separates them, is certainly one of the most awe inspiring scenes in Theo's rich filmography, and definitely among his finest in its organisation; and the very end shot, with the reporter in the bleak landscape, filled out with the dozen men in yellow coats mounting the cable poles, identical in their dress and timing (clearly a symbol of the importance of proper communication), is perhaps the most powerful image in the whole movie.

Theo got inspiration for his films everywhere he went. As for the wedding scene, it was inspired by the most unlikely of sights: "As for the marriage scene in *The Suspended Step of the Stork* with the bride on one side of the river, the bridegroom on the other – when I wrote the script, the scene was different, but I felt something was missing there. Then, one day, I was in New York on a bus going to Bronx through Harlem. At a stop, I saw a small black boy improvising some dance steps on one side of the street, and on the other side, there was another small black boy, who was answering him with his own dance steps. Nothing out of the ordinary, maybe, but I immediately saw the river in the middle..."

Those familiar with Theo's work might sense a little more direct emotion here, and anyone ready to throw the clichés that he is a cold filmmaker will maybe have to think again when viewing The Suspended Step of the Stork. As with The Beekeeper, these characters are carrying a lot with them. Though the main characters rarely address their fears and psychological weights, Karr's emotionally troubled reporter does openly question why he is in this place, and just what he expects to get out of it save a manipulative and journalistic angle of human suffering and displacement. His brief scene of externalised torment aside, Karr's character is both bogged down with the weight of his responsibilities and driven by a need for discovery, effectively a burden and a drive which often become too much for him. Mastroianni's enigmatic figure is similar to his mysterious Spyros in The Beekeeper, a man turning his back on it all but never really addressing to himself or anyone around him what exactly he is escaping and why he wishes to do so. But it is in the silence that one senses what he is running away from - himself, though of course as we all know one can never truly flee the person we are all destined to spend our lives with. Admirers of Marcello, and anyone aware of his rich past, will see that his work for Angelopoulos veers more towards his most sombre and existential work for the likes of Michelangelo Antonioni (La Notte). Of course he did carry emotional weight even in Fellini's lavish pictures - in La Dolce Vita, where he was torn between two worlds and a feeling of emptiness; and 8 1/2, as a tormented filmmaker out of inspiration - but those aware of his more typically charismatic performances (think Dark Eyes, Yesterday Today and Tomorrow, and much of his work for Ettore Scola) will see but a shadow or smudged reflection of the icon of Italian cinema. Here he embodies Theo's favourite type of figure, a man stuck between past and present, truth and fiction, life and death.

For Angelopoulos however, the main focus here was the idea of borders in a supposedly tight knit European Union. "We are talking about a united Europe, and yet today we are creating ever more borders," he later said when discussing the film and his career in general. "Borders which are so small they will soon be outside my home. The borders will be right outside my house. In a while I shall be a state. Me. For me the concept of borders has always been a concept which has generated strange associations, which has circulated and stimulated my thought. A dark, unexplored region. A concept of borders which was not just the geographical boundaries, but the limits of existence. The limits between life and death, the limits in love, the limits in language, in communication. Narrowing down the borders narrows down the communication, it stretches the differences, it magnifies the oppositions, it magnifies the causes of war, it magnifies the refugees, it magnifies internal exile."

The complex history of the Balkans goes back to the 1300s, and though Angelopoulos would never try to sketch out a history of the borders and territories of this region in a single film, he does commentate on it as only an artist can. (Some knowledge on Greek history certainly helps when watching Angelopoulos'

films, for there are many comparisons and allegorical connections between the two.) The border exists both literally and symbolically here, as a physical barrier to separate countries, to segregate human beings into categories, and as a line separating two realities, a past and a present. The Albanian/Greece border is Theo's focus here, but the border becomes a fitting hook on which we can hang questions of identity, what makes us one thing and not another, merely for the bit of land we are born on. When the Colonel hovers his right foot over the border, with opposing troops holding machine guns in view, he even says that one more step and he will be "somewhere else", adding after a pause, "or die". In one scene, Theo not only makes sense of the film's abstract title, but also defines the ludicrous nature of social division.

What is significant about The Suspended Step of the Stork, and perhaps what lends it an even greater sense of detachment, is the fact that screenwriter Tonino Guerra, one of the true greats of Italian film, was Theo's co-writer. They had worked together previously on Landscapes in the Mist and The Beekeeper, and in the future would co pen Ulysses' Gaze. European film buffs will know his name from some of Michelangelo Antonioni's masterpieces, like La Notte and L'avventura, as well as minor gems Zabriskie Point and Beyond the Clouds, not to mention his co writes with the great Federico Fellini, on Amarcord and Ginger and Fred in particular. Tonino also, funnily enough, wrote several films to star Mastroianni, unarguably the most prolific and important star of European cinema; including Casanova 70, The Voyeur, Enrico IV and Marriage Italian Style. Guerra helps lend the film the kind of melancholic ponderous nature which dominated and indeed enhanced the likes of The Beekeeper and Landscapes in the Mist. Clearly, Angelopoulos and Guerra were on the same page and tended to lean towards disconnected characters searching for answers and an escape from themselves.

It seems inevitable that, given the documentarian's detachment from the plain humanity of his subjects, the final meeting between Moreau and Mastroianni's characters, to determine whether he really is her husband, the politician in exile, that it should mostly not be seen through a human gaze, but on a screen as captured by a video camera. At the beginning of the film, as the team arrive in the refugee village, it is commented that the people there are lost in a kind of elsewhere which has become mythical. While they are stuck between locations, without anywhere to properly call a home, so too are the film crew, between the seams of recognising people on a human level and as subjects for the camera lens. One might think Karr's character captures the refugees' faces to immortalise their vulnerable humanity, when in fact he knows he is really only truly concerned with getting a good shot for himself as a filmmaker. Perhaps Theo saw a little of himself in this role, a man essentially capturing despair, disenchantment and misplacement within a creative medium in an artistically minded framework. That said, Theo is clear on how these people have become pawns in a political board game, how their humanity and very being is secondary to what they represent to the powers that be. They have ceased to be people, now only symbols of modern politics. But Theo certainly sees them as people. Marcello Mastroianni utters a line which is perhaps the most important in the whole film: "Being a refugee is an internal condition more than an external one." This considers the plight of the refugee from the viewpoint of the individual, not the observer. He concludes with "How many frontiers do we have to pass to get home?" This line, delivered by a tired man, embodies the exhaustion and helplessness of being a refugee, a person forever looked down upon but rarely given the chance to free himself of the shackles which keep him lowly.

Speaking to Andre Horton in 1992, Theo spoke of refugees: "Many nations, including Greece, are climbing over the bodies of murdered innocent people, most recently in Greece in order to make some political advantage. I want a new politics in the world with vision. It must be a new form of communication between people." Theo's words are inspiring, but given the state of the world now, his hopes of a more humane political structure seem more naive than ever. As I write, even during the coronavirus pandemic which shakes the whole world, there are refugees without a safe place to go, to protect themselves from the disease which threatens us all.

Like The Beekeeper, The Suspended Step of the Stork didn't receive quite as much acclaim as his other films, though it did garner some decent reviews. That said, unusually for Theo's work it didn't win any awards, earning only a

Palme d'Or nomination at Cannes in 1992.

In America it was not greeted as his finest work. The New York Times ran an underwhelmed review, stating, "His new film, The Suspended Step of the Stork, will be shown at the New York Film Festival tonight at 6:15 and tomorrow at 9:15 P.M., offering a high-profile opportunity for Mr. Angelopoulos. Unfortunately, this is neither his best work nor the best introduction to it.All the elements of a first-rate Angelopoulos film are here, from the political undercurrent to the sustained long-shots that are his trademark. As the camera pans slowly along a line of abandoned railroad cars in which refugees live, the film demonstrates that few directors use wordless images as purely or effectively as Mr. Angelopoulos. Yet the work suffers from a major, disastrous decision. Its centerpiece is the reporter, a bland, banal character unable to offer any intriguing perspective on the politician's identity. As played by Gregory Karr, this mournful-eyed journalist dissolves suspense wherever he turns. He can turn a silent, eyes-across-the table seduction into an unintentional parody of an Angelopoulos scene. Only when the film focuses on Mr. Mastroianni, who towers over everyone else here, does it capture the mystery, ambiguity and poignancy of this man's situation, whoever he turns out to be."

It is true of course that Mastroianni delivers the film's most impressive performance, but picking out one actor's work over another's seems to be missing the point. This is a film to taken in its completeness, in what it is saying about humanity, or rather the lack of it, as opposed to one performer outshining another. The truth is of course that each cast member, whether a walk on, a bit player or one of the leads does precisely what is needed of them to fulfil Angelopoulos' grand vision.

The Suspended Step of the Stork, it has been said, can be paired with Ulysses' Gaze as part of Angelopoulos' "Balkan Duo", for both are films which look at the after effects the history of the Balkans has had on 20th century people. Theo even links the two films together by including a clip of Suspended... at the start of Ulysses' Gaze, and by shifting the film's lone journeyman from a reporter to a filmmaker, played by Harvey Keitel at his most pensive. They are both films about a man on a journey, an inner and outer quest, directed by a man who declines to give us a history lesson but is adamant that Greece's history, and in particular its direct effects on future generation, remains a vital part of his filmmaking.

In one interview, Theo spoke of the individual filmmaker, the artist in the midst of an industry, and how The Suspended Step of the Stork was a statement which had to be made. "The world needs cinema now more than ever. It may be the last important form of resistance to the deteriorating world in which we live. Many write to me and say that The Suspended Step of the Stork was a film that had to be made because it captures so much of the tension today. You see, in dealing with boundaries and cultures today, the refugees who are homeless and not wanted, I am trying to seek a new humanism, a new way."

Though nearly thirty years on from the film's release this new way has not materialised, the chances are, even in the face of what we encounter in the 21st century, Theo would remain hopeful of big changes; which means of course that so should we. In this regard, The Suspended Step of the Stork is not a film of its time, speaking about a specific era and problem; it is a very valid and relevant piece, a statement from one of world cinema's most important voices. It should not be overlooked. But it is a sad film, even with its underlying hope, for though one hopes that such scenes of refugees will one day be a thing of the past, even the brightest optimist has to admit that, try as we may, the plight of such people will remain a reality for centuries to come.

END.

116